YO-BYL-973

"*Money Shot* is a winner. The plot is clever, the writing engaging, and the dialogue is like stand-up comedy."

Lynn Lott, author of
Seven Steps on the Writer's Path

"We've all dreamed of finding that million-dollar bottle cap, but is there a better place to do it than Las Vegas? As in *Dice Angel*, Rouff weaves a fast-paced page-turner of a story hopping with memorable characters and hilariously insightful commentary on Sin City. What a great read!"

Megan Edwards, author of
Roads from the Ashes

"Brian Rouff's witty first-person writing style is unique. Throw in Vegas as a backdrop and it's impressive. But toss in a million-dollar three-point contest and you've got a fascinating tale of hoop dreams for the average guy."

Cathy Scott, author of
The Killing of Tupac Shakur

"Rouff delivers another cleverly written, tight paced insider's look at Las Vegas. *Money Shot* is a pick-it-up, can't-put-it-down delight."

Charlene Austin,
Writer's and Reader's Network

Also by Brian Rouff

Dice Angel
ISBN: 0-9717148-1-9

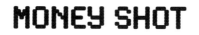

MONEY SHOT

MONEY SHOT

by
Brian Rouff

Hardway Press
Las Vegas, Nevada

MONEY SHOT

Published by Hardway Press
Hardway Press is an imprint of 21st-Century Publishing

Copyright © 2004 Brian Rouff

ISBN: 0-9717148-2-7

Cover Design: Alex Raffi
Interior Design and Production: Rachelle L. Rivers

1st Printing: September 2004

All rights reserved. No part of this publication may be translated, reproduced, or transmitted in any form or by any means, electronic or mechanical, including photocopying and recording, or by any information storage and retrieval system, without the written permission of the copyright owner.

AUTHOR'S NOTE

This book is a work of fiction. References to real people and organizations are used solely to lend the fiction a sense of authenticity and irony. All other characters and all actions, events, motivations, thoughts, and conversations portrayed in this story are entirely the product of the author's imagination. Any resemblance to actual persons or events is entirely coincidental.

DEDICATION

For Tammy

ACKNOWLEDGEMENTS

I'm grateful that so many people have given generously of their time and expertise in the development of this book.

To my first-readers:
The Usual Suspects—Trudy Altman, Steve Zieman, Bob Burris, Scott Brown, Kurt Lehman, D. J. Allen, Larry Wilde, Phyllis Beech, Frank Polak, Barry Rothstein. Thanks for always being there for me.

The New Kids—Lynn Lott, George Bergin, Amber Schutz, Lori Kozlowski, Elysha Long, Al Bernstein, Cathy Scott, Char Lyons. I owe you big-time.

To Deke Castleman, the best editor in the business (or any business). Thank you for not letting me settle for less.

To Rachelle Rivers, for making things easy.

To Alex Raffi, for another eye-catching cover.

To my daughters, Emmy and Amanda, who didn't think I was listening.

And to Tammy, for everything.

1

"You may already be a winner!"
"No purchase necessary."
"One pull can change your life!"
"Is that your final answer?"

Magic words, all. Seductive phrases that whisk us away to fantasyland faster than we can say "Publisher's Clearing House." Who among us is immune to their power? Not me, that's for sure. Hell, I live in Las Vegas, and I like to play cards, shoot dice, and pull handles the same as the next sucker. I even drive to California for the occasional lottery ticket. But until recently, I'd never won a blessed thing, unless you count those time share calls, always around dinner, that start, "Mr. Alan Nichols, I'm happy to inform you that you're the lucky recipient of ..." My personal-best hang-up time is 2.3 seconds.

Then Lady Luck waggled her finger in my direction. Not on the telephone, not in the mail, not in a casino, but in a completely unexpected way. A big-bucks bonanza from out of the blue (what a great name ... it's available for licensing; call me, we'll do lunch). A million-dollar windfall to wipe the slate clean and serve up the one thing we all really want in our heart of hearts. A fresh start. Something to make up for all the crap that life dishes out. The speeding tickets and the medical bills and the tax audits and all the other bad beats we don't deserve. Like my friend Jimmy, the congenial owner of the friendliest bar in Las Vegas, once told me, "If I ever hit the jackpot, I'd give half to my wife, and I'd be out the door for good. No questions asked." This was before she walked on her own, taking a lot more than half.

But that's a story for another time. As for me, Ms. Luck's favors came with a catch. Like the man says, "There's no free lunch." Still, I was able to scarf down plenty of complimentary appetizers before getting tossed out of the party.

It all started this past winter. I had just climbed out of the black hole of my annual post-holiday depression, a condition brought on by too little sunlight and too much credit-card debt. After many years, my wife and teenage daughter know to give me a wide berth until, one day, I wake up and no longer feel suicidal, just mildly nauseated. Then it's back to business at Dunbar and Associates, Vegas' biggest advertising agency, where I've toiled these last dozen years, first as copywriter, then as Account Manager, more recently hitting the wall as Director of Creative Services. That's me, one of the associates.

When I first started, I was thrilled just to be on the Dunbar team. In those days, I'd come home and tell my wife Pam, "I can't believe they actually pay me for this." It felt good to be rewarded for my creativity. I enjoyed playing with words, moving them around like little puzzle pieces until they all fit together seamlessly.

The problem was, I kept getting promoted. Which meant less time writing and more time bullshitting and babysitting, kicking butt and kissing ass. Today, my job consists of selling stuff nobody needs to people who don't know any better. Fuel the fires of American materialism. Brainwash John and Jane Q. Public into believing the latest exercise video, teeth-whitening gel, high-performance sports car or Italian designer suit is the only thing standing between them and hot monkey love. It's not something I'm proud of.

Don't get me wrong. Advertising's been good to me.

It's given me the money to buy a nice four-bedroom house in a quiet neighborhood, raise a family, and stay neck and neck with the Joneses, who are busy keeping an eye on the Smiths. All without having to shovel anything except hype, fix anything except bad grammar, or give back to the community in any conceivable way.

And, I'm good at it. I have the kind of brain that effortlessly cranks out clever little slogans that our clients are willing to pay actual money for. Lucky for me, I guess, because I have no other appreciable skills. Pam calls me a "savant," which is a fancy French word for somebody who does only one thing well. Like Rain Man, except not as good a driver. "If they ever drop the bomb," she says, "I'll have to leave you and find a real man. Somebody who can hunt and use tools. You have nothing to offer for the post-atomic age." I can't argue with that. They probably won't need an ad guy to come up with catchy copy to get us through the long nuclear winter. "Eat Fallout-Frosted Nuclies, the cereal with the shortest half-life." "Brush with Glow, now with Strontium 90." In case of attack, I'm leaving nothing to chance. I'll head straight for ground zero with a target on my ass.

I hit rock bottom earlier this year, when Dunbar asked me to personally pitch a new mob-themed casino called "Mugsy's." You know Vegas has come full circle when the "dese, dem, and dose" guys are once again all the rage. Not the real mob, who got bounced out on their cauliflower ears and went underground during the Howard Hughes era, but the gimmicky Disney-style mob of modern-day corporate America. Ironic, because the old-timers always say the town ran better and treated their clientele with more genuine respect before the Hiltons and Harrahs and Holiday Inns took over.

Now, you have to understand that Vegas needs another casino like I need a third mortgage. But Dunbar smelled easy money and that was that. Needless to say, I was less than thrilled and didn't give it my normal hundred and ten percent. Still, we threw together a cutesy Capone-like cartoon logo along with the following suggested themes: "We Got Your Casino Right Here!" "Tell Them Mugsy Sent You." And my personal favorite, "At Mugsy's, We Make You Feel Like a Made Man." Not exactly award-winning stuff, but, hey, this was spec.

So there I was at the big presentation, getting introduced to Mugsy's CEO Stephen Chapman and his gang of brown-nosers. Chapman, a cadaver-like character who looks like he mainlines chemo for the fun of it, has the personality of a liquid fart.

"Where's Dunbar?" he demanded, before I could even get settled in.

"Mr. Dunbar sends his regrets. He's a little under the weather today," I lied. Dunbar never goes to these things, unless they've got seven-figure potential. This wasn't even close.

"You've got ten minutes," Chapman grunted. "But I should warn you, we're changing the name of the casino."

Feeling tiny beads of flop sweat materialize on my forehead, I said, "Our whole campaign is built around the name."

"That's the breaks. The new name is 'Steve's.' My wife came up with it. Catchy, huh? She used to be in the ad biz back in Duluth."

"A hotbed of creative activity."

Chapman missed the sarcasm. "Show us what you've got, anyway," he said.

With even less enthusiasm than usual, I plowed through our dog-and-pony show. A couple of graphs and pie charts, the aforementioned slogans and logo, and a bare-bones media plan. Years ago, I learned not to divulge too much to prospective clients or they'd steal it and do it themselves. Not such a bad idea, come to think of it. When I wrapped up, Chapman said, "Not enough TV. I want to see us all over the goddamned tube."

"To be honest, you didn't give us the budget for ..."

"Horseshit!" he exploded, a burst of saliva grazing my forehead. "If you people would spend more time negotiating instead of bending over for every fucking station in town, we'd get the kind of coverage we deserve."

You'd think I'd be used to it. After all, second-guessing is second nature in this business. But I'd had more than enough. Gathering up my materials, I said, "We'll take that under advisement. Thanks for your valuable time." Not bothering to shake hands, I headed for the door. As I hurried through the lobby, I noticed Tim Sizemore, owner of the shlockiest ad shop in town. Sizemore is advertising's equivalent of the ambulance chaser. He never met a pitch he didn't like. God forbid he should service his existing clients. But after he's drained them dry, he somehow loses interest.

"Chapman's waiting for you," I told him. "You're made for each other."

On the way back to the office, I stopped at the nearest Speedee-Mart for a Bigg Fizz to settle my stomach. For those not on the cutting edge of pop culture, Bigg Fizz is a new soft drink whose competitive edge is "twice the carbonation of the leading brand." In advertising, we call that their "market position." You might call it an angle or gimmick. Either way, they're targeting teenage boys and middle-aged men. Basically, anybody in need of a really good burp.

Because of the work I'm in, I should pay attention to the ads on TV and radio. But sometime around my fortieth birthday, I stopped giving a damn. That's why I didn't understand the "You Win!" message on the inside of the Bigg Fizz bottle cap. Probably a free soda, logo gear or Burger King discount. Absent-mindedly, I tossed the cap on the car floor.

That was on Friday afternoon. I spent a gloomy weekend pondering my dead-end future and trying not to

upset my wife. Sometimes, when I'm particularly mo-
rose, she'll ask me what's wrong. Once, early in our marriage, I made the mistake of actually telling her. She cried
for two days. Lesson learned.

On Monday morning, I swung by Jason McBride's
apartment on the way to the office. Jason, one of our
hotshot young account executives, was having car trouble
and had called me for a ride. I had to laugh, because his
BMW Roadster is always in the shop, while my Toyota
Camry, now registering fifty-five thousand miles and
counting, is built like the Energizer bunny. Despite his
superficial love affair with fast cars, Jason's a good kid.
He kind of reminds me of me when I was first starting
out. Dunbar likes him, too. He makes Jason the point man
for all of our middle-aged female clients, who can't resist his curly blond hair and penetrating blue eyes.
Dunbar says that if Jason serviced his accounts in a G-
string, he'd pull in an extra five hundred grand a year.

Fortunately for me, Jason was wearing standard business attire.

"Dude, thanks for the ride," he said as he opened the
passenger door. Surveying the assorted debris on the floor
of my car, he added, "Hope I don't step on anything important."

"Nah, just kick it out of the way. Sorry I didn't have
time to clean up the mess."

"No problem. It's still better than the bus."

We settled into some innocuous shop talk during the
twenty minute drive to Dunbar's downtown digs, a converted ranch-style home nestled on a tree-lined street
between an attorney's office and a CPA firm. Originally
sub-divided in the 1930s, the one-time residential neighborhood has undergone a complete transformation over
the last decade. Our tastefully appointed office always
draws four-star reviews from clients impressed by one
of Las Vegas' oldest structures, a rarity in a town known
more for bulldozing history than for preserving it.

As we pulled into the parking lot, Jason's cellular phone slid off his lap and onto the floor. Reaching for it, he glanced at the bottle cap, picked it up, and did a classic double take.

"Whoa! Do you have any idea what this is?"

"It's a bottle cap," I said, mystified by his tone of voice.

"I mean, what kind of bottle did it come from?"

"Bigg Fizz, I think. What's the big deal?"

"The big deal is, you might have hit the freaking jackpot."

"Yeah right, with a bottle cap. Quick, call my real estate agent and tell her to buy that home on Mt. Charleston I've been dreaming about."

"I'm serious," he said, scrunching up his forehead. "Don't you watch TV?"

"Not if I can help it."

"Well, if this is what I think it is, you get to shoot a basketball for a million bucks."

"I don't believe in shooting innocent sports equipment," I said. "It goes against everything I stand for."

"Come on, call the eight-hundred number and see if I'm right." Sure enough, there was a toll-free phone number on the cap, directly under the "You Win!" message. I hadn't noticed it before.

"Okay, I'll call during lunch." Jason was probably full of crap and I didn't want to get my hopes up for nothing. Still, I was feeling a little excited, despite myself.

"Do it now, man," he insisted. "Here, use my phone."

"All right, hand it over. I'll give it two minutes."

I punched in the number, fully expecting to become mired in voicemail hell.

Instead, I was surprised to hear a pleasant female voice answer on the third ring, "Bigg Fizz Winner's Hotline. How may I help you?"

Taken aback, I stammered, "I'm not sure, exactly. My loser friend says I have a winning bottle cap."

Waiting for her to break out in howls of derisive laughter, I was again surprised when she said, "Do you have the cap in your possession?"

"My buddy has it, but I think I can beat it out of him. Hey, Slick, hand it over." He gave me the cap. "Okay, I've got it."

"There's a serial number at the bottom. Would you read it to me please?"

Squinting to make out the impossibly small numbers, I said, "'S' like in Simoleon, 'F' like in Filthy Rich, 1409-22."

The voice said, "Please hold the line." The happy strains of the Bigg Fizz jingle immediately filled my ears, ("Bigg Fizz, Bigg Fizz, it's the bubbles, that's what it is!") while I waited for whatever was going to happen next.

"What'd she say? What'd she say?" Jason asked impatiently. He looked like a kid getting ready to open his Christmas presents. I thought he might pee his pants any second.

"I'm on hold. She's checking."

After another two or three minutes and another resounding chorus by the fabulous Bigg Fizz singers, an authoritative male voice came on the line.

"Sir, may I have your name please?"

"Why, am I in some sort of trouble?" Jason punched me in the arm.

"Stop screwing around," he whispered.

"Not at all," the voice said. "We just need your name for our records."

"Alan Nichols." I spelled the last name.

"Congratulations, Mr. Nichols. I'm pleased to inform you that you're the winner of our Bigg Fizz Million Dollar Challenge."

"What does that mean, exactly? Does it involve time share?"

"I beg your pardon?"

"Never mind. It's just that I've never won anything,

except for a goldfish in third grade, and I'm a little skeptical. The fish died, by the way."

"I can assure you, this is perfectly legitimate." And with that, my benefactor told me what I had won.

After I hung up, Jason's voice pulled me back to reality. "Well?" he asked. "Was I right? Was I?"

I nodded slowly, still not believing it myself. "It seems I'm the halftime entertainment for the NCAA Western Region Championship Game on March 23rd. They're flying me and the whole family to Phoenix."

Jason was beaming as he gave me a high-five.

"Holy shit, that's unbelievable!"

"I get one chance to make a three-pointer. If it goes in, I'm an instant millionaire."

"What if you miss?"

"Fifty grand. Still not a bad day's work."

"That's for sure. I hate to ask, but are you any good?"

"Haven't picked up a ball since high school. Even then, I wasn't on the team. They didn't have much use for a clumsy five-foot-nine Jewish kid. Though my buddies and I used to play night ball at the park. Had to bring our own flashlights. Not that it made any difference."

"So, what are you gonna do?"

"I don't know. Practice, I guess. I have about four weeks to develop some serious game."

"I wish I could help, but I stink at hoops. Now, if it was surfing …"

"Yeah yeah, you're a real Moon Doggie."

"Who?"

"Forget it. Listen, you've helped more than you know. If it weren't for you, I never would've called."

"You're welcome."

"That's why I'm giving you ten percent."

His face registered genuine surprise. "You don't have to do that."

"I know, but it would make me feel good. I think.

You'd better take it before I change my mind."

"Thanks, man." He offered his hand and we shook to seal the deal.

"Besides," I asked, "how else are you gonna get your car out of hock?"

Before leaving, I swore Jason to secrecy. I thought it was better not to tell anyone for a while. Still, as I walked through the office, it was all I could do not to shout it out at the top of my lungs. Normally, I'm a fairly subdued guy. I tend not to get overly excited when my meager tax refund arrives or when my wife hits a $500 jackpot at the grocery store. (I never see that money, anyway. We have a typical arrangement. What's hers is hers, and what's mine is hers.)

But this was some serious cash, and not just a pipe dream, either. I was closer to a million-dollar lump sum than I'd ever been in my life. I couldn't wait to call home.

My eighteen-year-old daughter, Amy, answered the phone. I was surprised she was up before noon. As a UNLV freshman (known around these parts as the "13th grade"), her schedule leaves plenty of free time for partying and sleeping in. She has the best of both worlds: all the privileges of being an adult with none of the responsibility. Adult Lite. I have to admit, I'm jealous.

"Hi, honey, is Mom home?"

"I think so. What do you want?" she asked with that teenage girl attitude that starts somewhere around puberty and ends just after menopause.

"Are you screening her calls now?" I asked. Although I try to be civil, she has a way of making me insane.

"Be calm, I'll get her."

A few moments later, Pam picked up the line.

"What's up?" she asked sunnily. "Didn't you just leave a half-hour ago?"

"Yeah, but I've got news. Big news."

A long pause. "They finally fired you, didn't they?"

"No such luck." I proceeded to tell her about the

morning's events. When I was done, there was silence on the other end.

"Are you still there?" I asked.

"Sure. I was just thinking."

"About what?"

"About the wonderful man I married. I've got an idea."

"I'm listening."

"Why don't you take the rest of the day off and we'll figure out how to turn you into a basketball player."

"Does that include sex?"

"Not for the next four weeks."

"That's an old wives' tale."

"I'm an old wife."

"See you soon. Wear something naked."

"What will Amy think?"

"Give her a quarter and send her to the movies."

"It costs about fifty dollars these days, not counting popcorn."

"That's okay," I said. "We're gonna be rich."

"Always remember, I didn't marry you for your money."

"Good thing, since I made about twelve grand that year."

"Love you."

"Me too."

Suddenly, things were looking up. Amazing what the prospect of a cool million can do. I begged off work with a sudden "migraine" and headed for home.

2

Pam greeted me at the door wearing the dangerous red negligee that severely clouds my judgment. Even without makeup, she reminds me of the old ad campaign, "You're not getting older, you're getting better." Me, I'm just getting older.

"Let's see it," she said.

I began to unzip my fly.

"Not *that*," she laughed. "The bottle cap."

"Oh, that," I said, feigning my best hurt look. I reached into my pocket and produced the object of my affection, along with some lint and a stick of Double Mint gum.

Pam examined it for a moment before saying, "It looks so normal. I thought maybe it would be made of gold or something."

"It's better than gold."

Pulling me by the belt, Pam said, "Let's get you out of these work clothes. You'll think better when you're relaxed."

"What about the Princess?"

"I sent her to the mall with your Platinum Card."

"Damn," I said. "I'm gonna have to make this shot just to break even."

With Pam in the negligee and Amy at the mall, we took advantage of the situation. Twice. I try to do that once a year, usually on my birthday, just to see if I still can. The way I figure it, the day I can't is the day I'm officially old. I'll wake up one morning and have a sudden longing for Sans-A-Belt slacks and white patent-leather shoes. Until then, like the man who fell off the building said, "So far, so good." They wouldn't have to back the Viagra truck up to the house just yet.

When we were done, Pam stared at me a long time and finally asked, "So what are you going to do?"

"A nap would be nice."

"About the basketball."

I propped myself up on one elbow, the better to look at that still-tight body. No question, she was the same sun-drenched blue-eyed California girl I married more than twenty years ago. Golden, like the state itself back then. Nothing at all like the women I usually dated. A *shiksa*, my folks had called her, using the derogatory Yiddish term for a non-Jewish female. Of course, after they got to know her, they liked her better than me.

"Earth to Nick," Pam broke in.

Smiling, I said, "I guess I need two things: A place to practice and somebody to teach me."

"A coach."

"Yeah. Any suggestions?"

"What's Chuck Daly doing these days? Anybody who could handle Rodman can certainly put up with your nonsense."

"You're a big help."

"Well, why don't you call the local high school? Or the Y. They must know somebody who can work with a no-talent middle-aged white guy."

"Stop, I'm getting a big head."

We were interrupted by the sound of the doorbell. Reluctantly, I pulled on my pants and headed downstairs to see who dared interfere with my perfect day.

It was the FedEx man. I should have known, because Flash, our ancient black Lab who never barks at anyone (including burglars), was having a meltdown. I've never been able to understand why he hates the FedEx man so much. Was it the truck, or the uniform, or did he harbor a secret grudge against the whole organization? Just another of life's unsolvable mysteries. In the unlikely event I get to heaven, that's the first thing I'll ask.

I stepped onto the porch, careful not to let Flash out, and signed for the packet. Glancing at it, I was shocked to see the label from the Omni Corporation, makers of Bigg Fizz and a zillion other products we can't live without. Wasn't it just this morning that I had spoken to them? These guys were good.

Spreading the contents on the kitchen table, Pam and I examined the myriad release forms, disclaimers, and other assorted legal paperwork. "All decisions of judges final … blah blah blah … non-transferable … blah blah blah … hold harmless … blah blah blah … agree to appear in all advertising and promotional announcements … blah blah blah … acts of God … blah blah blah." ("It'll be an act of God if I make the shot," I told Pam.) I quickly signed the documents and enclosed them in the return envelope thoughtfully provided by my new best friends, the fine folks at Bigg Fizz.

"I guess it's official," Pam said. "I'm not sure I completely believed it until now."

"Do me a favor," I said. "Let's keep this under wraps for a while. I don't want every Tom, Dick, and Harry hitting us up for a loan. Especially the ones on your side of the family."

She smiled. "Just because they're borderline homeless, you think they'd ask us for money?"

"Call it a hunch."

"Oh, all right. Hey, isn't it time you got to work?"

"I took the day off, remember?" I said.

"I mean you'd better find a gym. Daylight's a burnin'."

I made a few phone calls and decided on the local rec center. I also left messages for potential coaching candidates. I hoped they wouldn't drag their feet.

After a quick detour to stick the bottle cap in our safety deposit box, I headed for the gym. The East Las Vegas Recreation Center is a modern facility, free to those who live in our little corner of the world. While most of our tax dollars go toward digging up the same street over and over for all eternity, the rec center is actually a rare example of money well spent. I'm embarrassed to say I'd only stepped foot inside once before, about two years ago when an ill-advised New Year's resolution sent me to the weight room with visions of bulging biceps and washboard abs. That lasted for exactly one long interminably boring session. By the time I was done, I felt like sticking my head in the weight machine and letting two hundred pounds of cast iron put me out of my misery.

But this was different. After checking in with the Heidi Klum look-alike at the front desk (yet another reason to hang around), I found myself on the basketball court. Instantly, the aromatic mixture of wooden floorboards and residual sweat transported me back twenty-five years to high-school gym class. I glanced around nervously, half-expecting somebody to pull down my shorts.

Luckily, at this time of day I was the gym's only occupant. I picked out a new Spalding indoor/outdoor official size and weight basketball from the rack and made my way to the three-point line.

The ball felt good in my hand. I bounced it once, twice, three times, the sound echoing off the gym walls. Why, I asked myself, hadn't I played in a quarter of a century? And, while I was at it, where did the time go, anyway? With an involuntary shudder, I snapped out of it. This was a non-productive line of thinking. I had a job to do. Staring at the basket, which seemed about a mile and a half away (not the NCAA's 19 feet, 9 inches ... I looked it up), I launched the ball. As if moving through Jello, it wobbled toward the front of the rim and fell harmlessly to the floor, about three feet short. Even worse, I felt a disturbing twinge in my shoulder. Letting the ball bounce out the door into the lobby, I attempted to lift my right arm. It hurt like hell. That would be the end of basketball for this particular day, at the very least. Not the auspicious start I was hoping for.

I retrieved my belongings from the front desk ("Done already?" Heidi asked cheerfully) and called Dr. John Holliday, my friendly neighborhood chiropractor.

3

Doc Holliday, a distant relative of the famous Western gunslinger (or so he claims; personally, I think it's a marketing ploy), has heard all the jokes before. Built like one of your larger NFL tight ends, the good doctor cuts quite an imposing figure as he spreads the Gospel of Chiropractic with more religious fervor than a dozen Jerry Falwells. "I'm the most compassionate doctor you've ever met," he once told me. "That's because I haven't used any of it yet." And sure enough, his tolerance for whining and moaning is lower than Hannibal Lecter's. Which is ultimately unimportant, because he's a natural healer of the highest order.

As soon as I walked into the examining room, I knew I was in trouble.

"Nichols, haven't seen you in quite a while," he barked. "What happened to that maintenance program I had you on?"

Sheepishly, I said, "You know how it is, what with one thing and another ..."

"Well, you're lucky I could squeeze you in today. That's usually reserved for my regular patients."

"Actually, I *am* lucky," I mumbled cryptically.

"So what's bothering you?"

I told him what I did to my shoulder.

"Basketball on a weekday afternoon," he harrumphed. "What's that, some midlife thing?"

"Sort of." Ordinarily, I would've wilted under his

withering look of disapproval, but now I could pull out my big gun.

When I finished telling him about the Bigg Fizz Challenge, he said "Congratulations," as he manipulated me into something akin to a half-nelson. The satisfying cracking sound meant either relief or paralysis.

"That ought to do it," he assured me. "I'm going to put you on a half hour of heat and muscle stim. Ice it down tonight, twenty minutes on, twenty off, and don't take any more ill-advised shots for a week."

"A week!" I protested. "I'm running out of time as it is."

Doc Holliday looked unimpressed. "Either that or risk serious damage. It's up to you."

"You're the doctor," I said glumly.

"And don't you forget it."

As I was buttoning my shirt, he added, "You know, I played a little college ball up at Weber State. A word to the wise. Always do your warm-ups."

"How'd it go, hotshot?" Pam asked as I dragged myself through the door.

"Don't ask," I said. "I took one three-pointer and hurt my shoulder."

"Bad?"

"I'll live."

"Did the ball go in?" she asked.

"No, it didn't go in," I said. "Gee, whatever happened to sympathy?"

"Sorry." She patted my hand twice. "There, there, poor baby. How's that?"

"A little enthusiasm would be nice."

"So, can you still play?"

"Not for a week, according to Doc Holliday."

Pam frowned. "Bummer. Didn't you warm up?"

"That's the same thing he asked me."

"I knew I missed my calling. Well, at least we'll have time to go over this list I made while you were out."

Immediately, the little warning light in my head flashed bright red. "List? What list?"

"Oh, just all the things I'll be needing after we're rich." She handed me a piece of yellow legal paper. On it, in her trademark handwriting that looks like calligraphy, were items ranging from a vacation cabin in Cedar City and a Toyota Land Cruiser to lasik eye surgery and new diamond earrings. Big ones, no doubt.

"Christ," I said. "No pressure, or anything like that. What about that abundant simplicity kick you've been on?"

She dismissed it with a wave of her hand. "Oh, that. That's for the middle class. Not for people like us."

"You're kidding, right?"

"Maybe. I can dream, can't I?"

Still frowning at the list, I said, "I notice there's nothing here with *my* name on it."

"Sure there is," Pam said, indicating a tiny entry near the bottom of the page. "See, right after my trip to the Hidden Valley Resort and Spa, it says 'new socks.' Those are for you."

"Gee, thanks, honey. You know, assuming I can even do this, a million dollars doesn't go as far as it used to. Especially after taxes." I paused a moment before adding, "And an additional ten percent."

Pam did a double take. I wasn't going to slip this one past her, I could tell. She jumped on it like a puppy with a new chew toy. "And exactly what ten percent are you talking about, mister?" she demanded.

I hemmed and hawed before saying, "The ten percent I gave to Jason McBride for telling me about the bottle cap." When her expression didn't change, I hurriedly added, "If it wasn't for him, I never would've called."

"You're awfully generous with my money," she said.

"*Our* money," I corrected her.

"Right."

"I was feeling really good," I continued. "It just came out."

"Well, it's coming out of your half."

"Sure, fine. Look, as much fun as this is, I have to get some ice on this shoulder. Think you could find some for me?"

She thought for a moment. "It's possible. For, let's say, ten percent."

"To the moon, Alice," I said. Luckily for her, I couldn't lift my arm.

I spent the rest of the afternoon trying to reach coaches from various local high schools, but wound up just leaving messages. It was the middle of their basketball season, after all, and my somewhat urgent need wasn't a priority to them.

That night, over dinner, we decided to break the news to Amy. We haven't always been Brady Bunch parents, but somehow our daughter was turning out all right. She was pulling decent grades in her classes and working part-time at the outlet mall. Through a large measure of good luck, as well as common sense inherited from her mother, she had managed to avoid most of the common teenage pitfalls, other than rolling her car and walking away without a scratch (which had made her a minor celebrity among the neighborhood boys).

"Your father and I have something to tell you," Pam said after we were settled in around the table.

"Oh my God, you're getting a divorce!" Amy said.

"We're not getting a divorce," I jumped in. "We have good news."

"Oh my God, Mom's pregnant!"

"Stop it," Pam said. "Nick, tell her already, before she has a nervous breakdown."

"Honey, I won a contest today. I have a chance to shoot a basketball for a million dollars."

"No way!" Amy said. "You got the winning bottle cap?"

"Does everybody know about this but me?"

"Duh. Maybe if you watched TV sometime you'd have a clue."

"Anyway, I'll be spending lots of time at the gym for the next month or so."

"That is so cool." Cool is one of those words that's made a big comeback. Except today's kids think they invented it.

"We thought you'd be excited," said Pam.

"Dad, if we're gonna have money, can I get a Jetta? And a new wardrobe?"

"What is it with you women?" I asked. "Haven't you heard, the best things in life are free?"

"You sound like my friend Jessica."

"Jessica's a smart girl," I said.

"Not that smart. She just got arrested for shoplifting."

After dinner, in between on-again off-again icings, I watched a meaningless college basketball game on ESPN2. On the TV screen, the three-point line didn't look so tough. Less than a foot, really. I dozed off somewhere in the third quarter and dreamt of basketballs stuffed with hundred dollar bills.

4

I awoke, still in my recliner, at sunrise. Pam had thoughtfully thrown a comforter over me and I'd slept like a man with no worries. Not even Amy's usual after-midnight front-door slam and bathroom clunking had stirred me. Moving the chair to its upright position, I cautiously tested my right arm. It felt sore, but better than I expected. Thank God for chiropractors and ice. If my luck held, I might be back in the gym by tomorrow.

In the meantime, there was still the matter of work. Suddenly, it seemed less important than ever. During last night's game, I had begun to formulate a plan, and now, over breakfast, I cautiously broached the subject with Pam.

"How would you feel if I took a leave of absence until this whole thing's over?" I asked, trying to act nonchalant as I missed the bagel and smeared cream cheese on my hand. "I have some vacation time coming, and I figure they owe me the rest, for my twelve years of faithful service above and beyond, etc., etc." I looked at her expectantly, trying to gauge her reaction.

"Funny you should mention that," she said. "I was going to suggest the same thing. I mean, what's more important than a million bucks? Certainly not the Goldblob account, or whatever you're pretending to do around there."

"Hey, this is my life's work you're talking about," I protested, secretly relieved that it wouldn't be a point of contention. "I thought I'd go in and talk to the old man first thing this morning."

"Just don't piss him off."

Saluting, I said, "I'll handle it with my usual diplomacy."

She gave me an unreadable look as I let Flash lick my hand clean. "That's what I'm afraid of."

As soon as I walked into our reception area, I knew something wasn't right. Maybe it was the ten-foot banner that said, "Drain it, Nick!" Or the way everybody yelled, "Surprise!" Obviously, McBride had ratted me out. I couldn't wait to have a word with that boy.

But for now, I had to graciously deal with the retinue of well-wishers and glad-handers. A few, I'm sure, were actually sincere, but most were secretly cursing me and their own lousy luck. "Alan Nichols, of all people," the thinking probably went. "What did that asshole do to deserve a break like this? It just proves there's no God." But what they were saying was, "Nick, you lucky bastard, way to go." That was from Cooper in accounting. And "Send us a postcard from the French Riviera." Nakamura in Creative. And "Why don't you leave that wife of yours and run away with me?" Tara in Traffic. Funny, she looked like she almost meant it. My first brief taste of money, the great equalizer. Before I could respond to any of them, I spotted Jason McBride hiding in the copy room.

"This is all your fault," I said after I worked my way through the crowd. "I thought we had a deal."

"They tricked me," he said.

"I can't wait to hear this one."

"Well, Riley asked me why I missed the deadline on the Fricken' Chicken campaign, and I said I'd been having a hard time concentrating ever since you won the chance at a million dollars."

"And Riley picked right up on that, did he?"

"Yeah, he's pretty sharp."

"I can certainly understand how you walked into his trap."

He flashed a lopsided grin. "You're not mad at me?"

"Nah. I love the smell of chocolate cake in the morning."

Just then, a massive python-like arm wrapped itself around my shoulder. The arm was attached to an equally massive body belonging to one Joe Dunbar, owner and patriarch of the firm bearing his name.

"Nicely done, Nick," he said in his low growl. "When you get a chance, let's talk."

I swallowed hard. "No time like the present."

"Good."

I followed him into his expansive office that's always reminded me of an upscale sports bar. Every inch of wall space is covered with UNLV Runnin' Rebel memorabilia, including his prized possession, an autographed picture of him standing next to legendary ex-coach Jerry "Tark the Shark" Tarkanian. The inscription reads, "To Joe, our biggest booster." Tarkanian may have been a cheater, but he was *our* cheater, and most of us were sorry to see him run out of town. Besides, Vegas loves a winner; it makes for great advertising.

At age sixty-five, Joe Dunbar looks more like the construction worker he once was, instead of Las Vegas' most prominent advertising executive. Remarkably, after more than three decades at the helm, he still has the fire in the belly and competitive drive of men half his age. His business philosophy is simple: Surround yourself with good people and let them do what they do best. It's one of the reasons I've stayed so long. Joe feels his time is better served on the golf course and at UNLV basketball games, where he rubs elbows with Las Vegas' most influential power brokers. "It's all about the juice," he likes to say. In local parlance, "juice" means the ability to get things done, based on who you are and who you know, whether it's procuring a last-minute suite at Bellagio for New Year's Eve or finagling a zoning variance for your best client with one phone call. The bronze plaque on his desk says it best. "Old age and treachery will overcome youth and enthusiasm." Yes, Joe Dunbar has it all, including a trophy wife nearly thirty years his junior, a cute little Texas gal named Bobbi Sue. And eighteen-month-old twin boys. As comedian David Steinberg once said, "It's God's way of going, 'Booga, booga!'"

Settling his huge frame into the leather chair behind his aircraft carrier of a desk, Joe asked, "So how's it feel to be one of the luckiest S.O.B.'s in Las Vegas?"

"I'll let you know after I sink the shot."

"Which reminds me," he said, "I took the liberty of writing up a press release. Nothing wrong with generating a little positive PR for the firm."

He slid a piece of paper in my direction. I pretended to study it a moment before saying, "Nothing at all."

"By the way, you probably don't know I was a pretty decent basketball player in my day. Played forward with Army Special Services after the Korean War. We were practically undefeated. Traveled all over the world, took on all comers. Would've stuck with it, too, if I hadn't blown out my Achilles' tendon. The reason I'm telling you this is because I'd like you to take some advice from an old man."

"You're not old," I said. When I felt like it, I could still kiss ass with the best of them.

Joe smiled. "Now write this down, or at least remember it. The three most important things are practice, practice, practice."

Seeing my opening, I said, "I'm glad to hear you say that. I only have a short time to get good at this, and I was hoping to take a leave of absence."

I studied Dunbar's face. He's a hard man to pin down, even after all my years working for him. In addition to his other skills, I'm sure he's a helluva poker player.

"Now slow down a minute, son," he said finally. "That's not exactly what I was driving at. I just meant you should spend a few hours a day on the court."

"With all due respect, I don't think that'll cut it. I need to treat this like a full-time job. After all, these kinds of opportunities don't come down the pike every day."

Dunbar chewed on his pen thoughtfully. The seconds ticked away on the "Area 51" wall clock behind his desk. At last, he said, "The problem is, I don't think we can spare you right now. We've got three new clients coming on board in the next few weeks, not to mention your pitch for the convention business. I realize nobody's irreplaceable, but you come pretty close. It's your own damn fault, if you want to know the truth."

I tested a smile. "I'm flattered, Joe, but my guys are up to speed on the new stuff."

"I'd still be more comfortable with you riding shotgun. You know they always throw us a curve or two. I feel very strongly about this, Nick. Now's not the time."

My face began to flush. I could see where this was heading, but felt compelled to play it out. Taking a deep breath, I said, "I feel strongly about it, too."

Dunbar sat up straighter in his chair. "Nick, this doesn't sound like you. You've always been a team player."

"That's right," I said. "Good old loyal Nick. Mr. Dependable. You can always count on me. Well, I've never asked for a single thing and this is where it gets me."

"You might want to change your tone." Dunbar's voice took on a threatening note of its own.

"Or what? Loyalty's a two-way street, Joe, and I don't see anything headed in my direction."

When he didn't reply, I added, "Maybe it's time I picked up my toys and went home."

At last, he said, "If that's your attitude, maybe it is. Funny how the prospect of a few dollars changes people."

"The money has nothing to do with it." I stood up to leave.

"Nick," Dunbar said softly, "if you walk out that door, don't bother coming back."

I tightened my grip around the handle and pulled.

Dunbar's expression was a combination of sadness and resolve. "I'm sorry this has to end badly."

I looked at him and said, "Everything ends badly."

As the door clicked shut, the still-assembled crowd of now ex-coworkers launched into a spirited rendition of "For He's a Jolly Good Fellow." The irony was not lost on me.

I took the long way home, waiting for my heart rate to return to normal, playing and replaying my conversation with Joe a hundred times. There were many places where I could have backed down and I'd still be gainfully employed. But I just didn't have it in me. That was a game for a younger man, someone not closing in on critical burnout at warp speed. Although I was now out of a job for the first time in my adult life, I felt strangely buoyant, even giddy, like a schoolboy hearing the last glorious bell signaling summer vacation. Maybe this is what happens right before you snap, I thought. After a dozen years at Dunbar, all I could think of was, "I'm glad that's over." What a great epitaph that would make. Carve it on my tombstone: "I'M GLAD THAT'S OVER."

I rolled down the window and, hesitating just slightly, tossed out my cellular phone. It made a satisfying crunching sound as it skittered across the street right into a storm drain. At least there wouldn't be any more inane conversations about rate plans in my immediate future. "I have the Platinum Plan. Twelve hundred minutes a month for

$99. How about you?" "Oh, I *live* on my cell phone. They're putting together a custom plan just for me." Yeah, but my antenna is bigger than your antenna. Recently, I witnessed four young businessmen in custom suits and power ties having lunch at Café Nicole, one of Las Vegas' more fashionable bistros. All of them were on their cell phones. For all I knew, they were talking to each other.

5

For the second time in two days, I came home early.

"This can't be good," Pam said as I tossed my suit jacket over a chair.

Smiling weakly, I said, "It depends on your definition of good."

We poured iced teas, sat at the kitchen table where we'd had so many other important discussions, and I told her what happened.

When I finished, Pam said, "I'm confused. Aren't you supposed to quit your job *after* you win the million dollars?"

"Technically, yes. But things sort of spun out of control. Look on the bright side. I need all the practice I can get." I paused before asking the critical question. "Are you mad at me?"

Pam looked thoughtful. "No, not angry. Just disappointed. I wish you'd handled it differently, that's all. You know I don't believe in burning bridges."

"I know."

"Do you think you'll change your mind in the morning?"

"I doubt it. But even if I did, I'm sure Joe wouldn't take me back. He's more pig-headed than I am."

"What do we do now?" she asked. A look of panic darted across her face and I felt a sudden twinge of guilt.

"Well, there's still the million-dollar shot. Even if I miss, that's fifty G's. Plus, I'm getting lovely parting gifts from the firm. Vacation time, sick days, severance maybe. We'll be fine." I hoped I sounded more confident than I felt. For the first time since leaving the office, I was beginning to have second thoughts. "And," I added, "if the shit really hits the fan, you can always go back to running cocktails at the Landmark."

Pam shook her head, a smile lighting up her sweet face. "They blew that place up years ago, remember?"

"Oh, right, it's a parking lot. Well, valets make better money, anyway."

I ducked the wadded-up napkin that whizzed past my head.

My shoulder was now about ninety percent better. I've always been a fast healer, like Schwarzenegger in the *Terminator* movies, back when he was still just a bad actor. My plan was to return to the gym as soon as I made a few phone calls. Coach Bobby Clark from Paradise High had tried to reach me while I was busy quitting my job, so that was my first order of business. He picked up on the second ring.

"Clark here," he snapped, sounding just like every other coach I'd ever spoken to.

I briefly introduced myself and explained my situation.

"Well, Mr. Nicholson, you've come to the right place," he said. "I guarantee I can turn you into a three-point machine in no time."

"Good to hear," I said, not bothering to correct his mispronunciation of my name. If he was the real deal, he could call me Charlie Manson for all I cared. "How much do you charge?"

"That's the sixty-four dollar question," he said. "Seeing as how I've never done this, one-on-one like, I'd have to give it some thought." He paused for less than three seconds. "How's about twenty-five hundred dollars a week and thirty percent of any endorsement money, plus all travel expenses and one fifty per diem? I can have my attorney draw up the contract and start working with you as early as, let's say, a week from tomorrow."

"Well, coach, I've never done this before either. Why don't I give it some thought and get back to you." *In like three decades*. I hung up. Coach Clark would have to find himself another meal ticket.

Before I could make my next call, the phone rang. It was Jason McBride.

"Hey, bud, how you doing?" he asked. "I just heard. We all did. I'm really sorry."

"Don't be. Things have a way of working out."

"You never even cleaned out your desk. Can I bring your stuff over?"

I was genuinely touched. You never know who your real friends are. Usually, they're not who you think.

"Nah, don't bother. Take what you want and stick the rest in that dumpster out back."

"Even the Addy awards?"

"*Especially* the Addy awards. They're not even for my best work. Those judges don't know their asses from third base."

"If you say so. I gotta tell you, though, we're gonna miss you around here."

"Thanks, Jason. Maybe we can get together this weekend, have a few beers, shoot the shit. Anything but talk shop."

"I'll give you a holler."

Suddenly, I wasn't in the mood to make any more calls. I headed for the bedroom to change into my gym clothes. On the way out, I passed Amy in the hall.

"Dude, tell me you're not leaving the house like that!" she said, her jaw dropping in horror.

In the good old days, the term "dude" was reserved for, well, guys of the male persuasion. Now, it's an all-purpose word for friends, teachers, dad, mom, the dog, anybody. I guess it makes life easier, not having to remember all those pesky names. I used to be offended, considering it a sign of disrespect, but had recently come to accept it for what it is. Just another verbal tic and devaluation of good diction.

Despite my better judgment, I took the bait. "Leaving the house like what?"

"Your shirt and shorts don't even match."

"Sure they do," I said. "They're both green."

Amy rolled her eyes. "Forest green and emerald green. You look like a giant booger."

"Maybe I'm a trend-setter. Listen, I'm just going to the gym. Nobody cares how I look. I'll probably be the only one there."

"You're hopeless!" she said, exasperated at my lack of fashion savvy. "That settles it. I'm doing some serious shopping for you this weekend. You're not going to embarrass me on national television."

"That's half the fun."

As I kissed Pam goodbye and walked out the front door, I heard Amy yell, "And pull down your socks!"

Once again, the gym was practically deserted. I checked in with Heidi, grabbed a ball, and took a little ten-foot jump shot. It clanked off the front of the rim, but at least my shoulder didn't hurt. Retrieving the ball, I noticed a black woman shooting alone at the other end of the court. Mid-twenties, about five-foot-six, muscular legs, very compact. She wore skin-tight bike shorts and an Everlast T-shirt. Her face reminded me of a bust of Cleopatra I had seen once in an encyclopedia. I inched closer and stopped to watch as she sank half a dozen free throws in a row.

"Nice stroke," I said, doing my best Dickie V impression.

"Thanks," she replied, not looking my way as the ball again found the bottom of the net.

I tried again. "Come here often?"

"No." The perfectly shot ball made a satisfying whapping sound.

"Me neither. It's just my second time."

She stopped and stared at me. "Mister, I hate to be rude, but I'm having a bad day, and I just want to be left alone."

Embarrassed, I mumbled, "Sure, no problem. Sorry." I started to retreat, then made one last attempt. "Do you mind if I sit here and watch for a while? I won't bother you, I promise."

"Suit yourself."

I positioned myself unobtrusively on the bottom bleacher and tried to carefully observe her technique, which appeared flawless. After making nine more free throws, the tenth rimmed out and rolled in my direction. I picked it up and passed it into her outstretched arms.

"Thanks," she said, turning back to the foul line. After taking a few steps, she pivoted and said, "Okay, I give up. What's so damned interesting about watching me shoot free throws?"

"I'm trying to learn and you look like you know what you're doing."

"Excuse me, but aren't you a little old to be hanging around the rec center in the middle of the afternoon? Someone might mistake you for a child molester."

"Yeah, you caught me. When does the school bus show up?"

She fixed me with a puzzled expression and said, "You're crazy."

"I know. But I need to work on my shot and I don't have much time. What's your secret?"

"Simple. You know Shaquille O'Neal?"

"Of course. Everybody knows Shaq."

"Just watch what he does and do the opposite." Her hearty laugh was infectious. I couldn't help but join in.

"My name is Alan Nichols," I said, extending my hand. "My friends call me Nick."

Taking my hand firmly in hers, she said, "Angela Jackson."

"A pleasure. So where'd you learn to shoot like that?"

"University of Detroit. I was the two guard for three years. Senior All-American."

"No kidding."

"We were good. Went to the women's Sweet Sixteen before getting upset by Cincinnati on a last-second prayer in double OT. That game still gives me nightmares."

"Why haven't I seen you someplace like the WNBA?"

She pointed to a ragged looking scar on her right knee. "Torn ACL. I tried to rehab, but never got it back. I just don't have the quicks for the pro game. Besides, that's ancient history."

"What do you do now, besides shoot free throws?"

"Until about three hours ago, I was a nurse at Meadows Hospital. They fired my ass, along with a bunch of other new hires. Cost cutting, they said. Hell, we couldn't keep up with the workload as it was. Let me tell you, if you ever get sick, stay away from that place. There's a reason it's across the street from a cemetery."

"I'll keep that in mind."

"This town's been nothing but heartache since I got here. My Aunt used to sing this song, 'Been Down So Long, It Looks Like Up to Me.' I'm starting to understand what she meant."

"You probably won't believe this, but I lost my job today, too. Quit, actually."

"For real?"

"I needed some time off and they wouldn't give it to me. First thing I ever asked for in twelve years."

She frowned. "That's how it goes sometimes. Treat us all like a damn piece of meat."

"You know what? I don't care. It gives me more time to work on my shot."

"What's up with that, anyway? You one of those mid-life crisis guys I been hearing about?"

That's when I told her about the Bigg Fizz Challenge.

As I was filling her in, a light bulb began to flicker somewhere in my head. Sometimes, I'm not the brightest guy in the world, but this one seemed obvious.

"You believe me, don't you?" I asked when I was done.

"I think so. You're either telling the truth or you're completely wack."

"Let me put my money where my mouth is," I said. "Here's a business proposition for you."

Her eyes locked onto mine. "I'm listening."

"Teach me how to shoot like you do. Work with me every day. Be my coach. I'll pay you a thousand a week against ten percent of my winnings."

Angela raised one eyebrow. "Sounds too good to be true."

"I know. But take a chance. It's gotta be better than picking up urine samples."

She didn't answer right away. At last, she said, "Okay. But if you're jerking my chain, I'll make it so you can't have kids."

"You're a little late for that. About eighteen years late."

We shook hands, agreeing to meet at ten the next morning. "Don't forget your checkbook," she reminded me. "None of that post-dated shit, either."

On the way out, she gave me my first homework assignment.

"Stop at the sporting goods store and buy a leather

game ball. Not like these phony balls here at the gym. Real ball has a whole different feel. Cost you about sixty bucks. Start carrying it around wherever you go. Get used to it, how it fits in your hand. Like a little kid with a new baseball glove. Even take it to bed with you."

I laughed. "I don't think my wife will appreciate that."

Her eyes twinkled as she said, "Tell her it's one of those new marital devices. It'll make her feel like a million bucks."

6

I walked into the kitchen with my new Wilson Official NCAA leather game ball.

"Meet my new friend," I said to Pam. "We'll be spending plenty of quality time together."

"Should I be jealous?"

"Maybe. There's something about the smell of real leather that makes me horny."

Pam put a finger to her lips. "Shhh, Amy's in the other room."

When Amy was little, Pam and I could make suggestive comments that went right over her head. "What's for dessert?" I'd ask.

"You'll get your dessert later," was her standard reply.

But now, anything remotely smacking of marital relations freaks Amy out.

"I know you guys still do it," she told us once. "I just don't want to know when."

Fair enough. So I lowered my voice and said, "All I can say is, I see a threesome in our future. You, me and Ms. Wilson here."

"Oh, brother."

"Coach's orders."

It took a second to sink in. "You found a coach?" she asked with genuine delight.

"I sure did," I said proudly. If I'd had an apple, I would've polished it on my shirt.

"What's his name?"

"That's a sexist comment. My coach happens to be a *she*. Angela Jackson. Ex-college player, Cleveland or Detroit or one of those places. The sweetest shot you'll ever see."

"How'd you meet her?"

"She was just hanging around the gym, shooting baskets and ..." I stopped in mid-sentence.

"What's wrong?" Pam asked.

"I'm an idiot."

"I know. Why?"

"I never even got her phone number. What if she doesn't show up for our appointment tomorrow?"

Pam put her hand on mine. "She'll be there. Have a little faith."

"I guess you're right."

"Did you discuss money?"

"Yes."

"And?"

"Promise you won't hurt me."

Pam gave me one of her famous looks. "You didn't."

"I'm afraid so. A thousand a week against ten percent."

Her eyes grew wide. "Are you nuts? What's with you and this ten-percent business? Talk about giving away the store. While you're at it, why not give ten percent to Doc Holliday and ten percent to the guy who sold you the basketball and ten percent to the reporter who called and ..."

"Reporter? What reporter?" I asked, happy to be changing the subject.

Pam thrust a piece of paper in my general vicinity: Jennifer Santiago, Channel 8 Action News. "She read about you in a press release and wants to do a story. Human interest. She obviously doesn't know you."

"Just what I need. Some talking head following me around, mucking up the works." I balled up the paper and threw it toward the wastebasket. It went in and out.

"Not a good sign," I said, trying to back out of the kitchen in one piece.

"Not so fast. You haven't heard the last of this ten-percent thing," Pam said. "Well, it's no skin off my nose. I don't care what you do; I'm keeping my half. I can see it all now. You'll be one of those work-for-food guys and I'll be living in a beautiful estate in Spanish Trail."

"Will you rent me a room? I'll help around the house."

"You don't help now."

"Sure I do. Every daylight savings, I reset the clocks."

"Big whoop."

"Fine. Be late for everything, see if I care. And another thing, next time there's a nasty old spider in the bathtub, handle it yourself."

"Don't think I won't. I'll hire a live-in exterminator. One with a big …"

"Hey," I interrupted. "Do you really think I should give ten percent to Doc Holliday?"

Before Pam could take a swing at me, I headed for the relative safety of the den. Maybe I could catch a game before dinner.

7

On Wednesday, I arrived at the gym promptly at ten o'clock. To my relief, Angela was already there, shooting baskets.

"Morning, Coach," I said.

"Morning."

"Look," I said proudly. "My own ball."

She examined it approvingly. "Nice."

"Here, I brought you a piece of paper with your name on it." I handed her a check for a thousand dollars. She studied it carefully, folded it in half and stuck it in her shorts pocket.

"Thanks," she said, throwing me the ball. "Let's see what you got."

It wasn't much. I moved to the free throw line and lobbed the ball up. We both watched as it ricocheted off the backboard, nowhere near the basket.

Angela frowned. "That's probably the worst shot I've ever seen. Didn't you play when you were a kid?"

I shrugged.

"Is it too late to ask for a raise?"

"Only if you want my wife to kill me."

"All right, pay attention. We got a lot of work to do. My college coach used to talk about the four C's: Confidence, Concentration, and Conceptualization."

"That's three C's. What's the fourth?"

"Cash." Angela gave me a high-five. "That's good, shows you're listening. We better start with confidence.

Stand over here." She indicated a spot about three feet from the basket.

"I can make this," I said.

"You think so? Go for it."

I shot and missed.

Angela tilted her head and looked at me appraisingly. "Are you sure you're right-handed?"

"All my life."

"Too bad, I thought I was on to something." She picked up the ball and said, "Now watch and learn."

She flicked it toward the hoop. It sailed through, nice as you please.

"The goal is for you to make ten of these punk-ass sissy shots in a row. That builds confidence. But first, we gotta develop some technique. You're all messed up."

"Sorry."

"You can't help it. It's a white thing."

"That's not politically correct," I said, pretending to be offended. "There're plenty of good white basketball players."

"Name three."

I hesitated a moment before saying, "Bird, West, Maravich."

"Retired. Retired. Dead. Besides, they had to work extra hard. Not as hard as you're gonna work …"

"Thanks."

"Hey, lucky for you I'm DWC."

"DWC?"

She smiled mischievously. "Down With the Crackers."

"Great, my coach is a racist."

"No," she said, still grinning. "*We* can't be racist. We're the *victims* of oppression, remember?"

"Maybe, but I'm the one feeling oppressed right now."

"Honey, you ain't seen nothin' yet."

Angela was right. For the next two hours, we worked

on my mechanics from the top down. Rest the ball on my finger pads, not on the palm. Put my index finger on the center of the ball. That's the shooting finger, the last one to come off the ball. Keep my elbow straight, perpendicular to the rim, forming a "T." Now move it five degrees to the right, so it doesn't block my line of sight. Shoot the ball, don't push it. Move my left hand, the one that guides the ball, slightly forward. Relax, be more comfortable. (Yeah, right.) Keep my wrist loose, so I can snap the ball and get some backspin on it. When I release the ball, keep my hand up and index finger out for a fraction of a second. That's the "follow-through freeze." Keep my eyes on the front of the rim. After I release the ball, watch it as it heads toward the basket. Don't shoot so flat, give it higher arc. It's more forgiving.

Which is more than I can say for my coach. She was tougher than a constipated drill instructor. By the time we were done, my brain felt like it was encased in solid lead. But I was making the majority of those three-foot "punk-ass sissy shots." And I'll be damned if I wasn't feeling a little more confident. Naturally, that didn't last long.

"I had no idea there was so much to learn," I said.

"We're just getting started," Angela replied. "Be thankful we don't have to work on ball handling, passing, rebounding, and dribbling."

"You're telling me."

"Tomorrow, we'll review. Then we'll focus on body control and footwork. In the meantime, I'm going to lunch. You can't leave until you make ten in a row. No cheating." She sashayed toward the exit, effortlessly spinning the ball on her index finger like a female Globetrotter. Once a jock, always a jock, I thought. If we ever had the time, maybe I could get her to teach me that move.

"Yes, ma'am!" I shouted after her. "Scout's honor!"

It's a good thing I was never a scout, because nine straight was the best I could manage. The first five were easy, but as I got closer and closer the pressure began to mount and I found myself tightening up. "You're a choker," I berated myself, not helping matters any. Well, that was one more thing I'd have to deal with. Tomorrow.

I cursed myself again for getting on the freeway instead of taking the surface streets home. Traffic was bumper to bumper, another symptom of Las Vegas' dubious status as the fastest growing city in America. When we moved here in 1987, it was to escape the traffic, smog, crime, and other charms of the City of Angels. Over the years, every one of them had followed us out. It made me sorry I left my forwarding address. On the plus side, we now had In 'N' Out Burger. As Emerson or Thoreau or one of those guys once said, possibly while wolfing down a Double/Double with cheese, "Life has compensations."

By the time I got home, it was already 4:25. The house was empty except for Flash, who half-heartedly wagged his tail, but didn't bother to get up from his usual spot. Even a year ago, he would have been a one-dog welcoming committee, but those days were over. Lately, I considered buying his dog food one can at a time.

Amy was at school and Pam wouldn't be done with her volunteer work at Grant-A-Wish for another hour. I didn't have the energy to even open the mail. Peeling off my T-shirt, I trudged upstairs and turned on the shower, waiting impatiently for it to heat úp. The steaming needles of water felt good on my aching muscles and I stayed in until it began to cool off. Hot showers are a luxury in a house monopolized by females. Whenever I rattle the door and tell Amy to hurry, she always has the same answer, even after an hour. "I'm washing the conditioner out of my hair."

Feeling almost human again, I pulled on my favorite cotton sweatshirt and a pair of ratty jeans, stopping briefly to stare at the rack of suits and dress shirts occupying an entire section of the walk-in closet. When was the next time I'd have to worry about what to wear to work? If I played my cards right, or more accurately, my Wilson Official NCAA ball, the answer was *never*. I looked forward to the day I could drop them off at the local Opportunity Village store, freeing up valuable closet space for a nice new assortment of Hawaiian shirts.

We ordered pizza for dinner. Over bites of zesty pepperoni and garden-fresh mushrooms (that was the copy writer in me), I told Pam about my first day at the "office."

"Angela's a great coach," I said. "But it's like any new skill. I have to think about each element, one at a time. Like when I first learned to drive a stick. Eventually, it'll become automatic. I hope."

"It sounds like you made the right choice."

"I'm keeping my fingers crossed. Except when I'm shooting."

"Well, I think we should have Angela over for dinner sometime soon. It never hurts to butter up the teacher."

Or your wife. Pam and I went to bed early. The basketball spent the night on the floor.

8

Morning came too quickly. I climbed out of the rack, careful not to wake Pam, who stirred briefly before resuming her normal rhythmic breathing. (That's what *she* calls it. I call it snoring.) Instantly, my body began to protest the previous day's activities. Especially my wrist, which hadn't been that sore since junior high. Tiptoeing downstairs, I decided to whip up a nutritious high-protein breakfast to help me face my new regimen. A nice cheese omelet would be just the ticket. For years I stayed away from eggs, based on my doctor's advice. The standing joke at our house was that my cholesterol was so high, my doctor had a heart attack. Lately, the medical community had done a complete turn-about on eggs, which were back on the approved list. Oddly, the more eggs and other protein I consumed, the lower my cholesterol dropped. That's why I no longer go to the doctor.

The omelet was delicious, one of the few holdover skills from my bachelor days. As I was clearing the table, Pam stumbled, bleary-eyed, into the kitchen, a pillow mark creasing her right cheek.

"How ya doin'?" I asked as I plopped a peanut butter sandwich into a Ziploc bag, watching with approval as the strip turned green. Whoever invented the Ziploc, much like the person who developed the no-lick stamp, should win a Nobel Prize.

"Do you have any chips around here?" I asked.

Stifling a yawn, Pam said, "Sometimes you make it

sound like you don't even live in this house."

"I know. So, do you?"

"They're right where they always are, in the third drawer next to the stove."

"Thanks." I opened the drawer and removed an individual bag of vinegar chips. "What a great selection. I guess I should visit more often."

"Be sure to leave a dollar. What's with the brown bag, anyway?"

"It's part of my new austerity program. I am, after all, unemployed."

"Oh, puh-leeze."

"Well, if you must know, I didn't get lunch yesterday, thanks to Angela. A world-class athlete like myself needs his nutrition."

"Good point. We can't have you fainting from hunger in the middle of your workout."

"So," I asked, "do you have any cookies?"

I decided to forego my usual morning shower and head straight for the gym. Luckily, Amy wasn't up yet, or I would have gotten an earful about the importance of good personal hygiene at all times. She never leaves the house, even to get the mail, without looking her absolute best: clothes coordinated and ironed, makeup perfect, every hair in place. Of course, her goals are slightly different than mine. I'm not hoping to meet boys. Still, in deference to my sleeping daughter, I pulled my cleanest dirty shirt out of the laundry basket.

Once again, Angela was waiting for me. I found her sitting on the bottom bleacher, sipping a cup of coffee.

"Where's mine?" I asked pleasantly.

"At the 7-Eleven," she said, all business. "How you feelin'?"

"Not bad for an old guy."

"We'll see about that. I want you to start with some stretching. Can't have you popping something you might need."

We went over some basic exercises designed to help me loosen up.

"Don't bounce," she instructed. "Just take it slow and easy."

After about ten minutes, she pronounced us ready to go.

"Stand here," she said. It was about halfway between the free throw line and the basket.

"Hey, I'm moving up in the world," I said.

"Show me what you remember from yesterday."

I went over my mental checklist. Finger-pad control. Elbow straight. Left-hand support. Flexible wrist. Eyes on the rim.

Angela's voice interrupted my routine. "You gonna take all day?"

"I'm thinking."

With that, I shot the ball, being sure to remember my follow-through. It dropped right through the center of the hoop.

"How's that?" I asked proudly.

"Not bad."

"Not bad? It was perfect!"

"Your elbow was too far out. Tuck it in closer to your body."

"Like this?"

"Exactly. Now, look at your feet. Where are they?"

They were side by side.

"I want you to put your right foot slightly in front of the left, maybe three inches in front, and move your feet shoulder-width apart."

I followed her instructions.

"Also, work on flexing your knees. It doesn't matter so much on these short shots, but that's where your power comes from, your legs. Try it."

I flexed a few times. My knees made their usual cracking noises. Angela winced.

"When you shoot, release the ball at the top of your knee flex. Don't work against yourself. You want everything moving in the same direction."

Again, I shot the ball. Smoother, but it fell short. "Shit," I said.

"No, it's all good," Angela reassured me. "You looked much better."

"I'm getting style points? I thought the object was to put the ball in the hole."

"No, the object is to have perfect mechanics every time. If you do, the ball will take care of itself."

"Kind of like Zen."

"That big Chinese guy?"

"You know, Zen. The religion. Or maybe it's a philosophy."

"I don't care if it's a hip-hop group. If it'll help you make a basket, I'm down. Go ahead, try again."

This time, the ball clanked off the back of the rim.

"What'd I do wrong now, Coach?"

"Look at your head."

"That's kind of tough to do, isn't it?"

For the first time that morning, Angela smiled. Maybe the coffee was kicking in.

"What I mean is, your head's crooked."

"It's genetic."

Angela sighed. "I'm gonna whup your smart ass."

"Yes, ma'am."

"Just be sure to keep your head straight at all times. If you do that, the rest of your body will be squared up toward the basket. Got it?"

"Got it."

"Now, take a hundred shots. I'll rebound."

I started out strong, making seven in a row, alternated misses for a while, faded down the stretch, and finished by sinking my last eight. The whole time, Angela barked out instructions like a New York traffic cop, reminding me to make this or that adjustment. When all was said and done, I hit at a fifty-eight percent rate, not too shabby for a guy who couldn't buy a shot three days before. I was also breathing noticeably hard.

"Listen to yourself," Angela said. "You're in some kinda terrible shape."

I was still breathing too hard for a snappy comeback.

"What sort of job did you say you had?"

"Advertising."

"Not a lot of heavy lifting, huh? When's the last time you got some exercise?"

"Does watering the plants count?"

"Go take ten laps around the gym."

"You're kidding."

"Do I look like I'm kidding?"

Rather than face the wrath of Angela, I did as I was told. Within thirty seconds, I remembered why I didn't ask if running counted. In fact, it ranks right down there with painting the house and visiting my wife's family in Poughkeepsie. By the time I staggered across the imaginary finish line, where Angela was filing her nails, my feet hurt, my lungs burned, and I had one of those horrible side aches that took me back to high-school gym class.

"I hate you," I wheezed, crouching with my hands on my knees.

"Good. Keep you on your toes."

"That's the last place I want to be right now."

"Take five and we'll finish up with some more shooting drills."

I hobbled off to get some water and wolf down my peanut butter sandwich. Out of the corner of my eye, I thought I saw Angela slowly shaking her head.

My break was over all too quickly, and then it was time to take another hundred shots. This time, Angela suggested I move about six inches to the left of my previous position, ensuring that my right arm lined up directly in front of the rim. With that simple adjustment, my success rate increased to sixty-four percent.

"That's enough for one day," Angela pronounced. They were some of the sweetest words I'd ever heard. "You're making progress."

"Really?"

"I wouldn't say it if it wasn't true. Now listen up. I'm going to drop some knowledge on you. It's the most important thing of all, like a trade secret. My daddy told it to me when I was a girl, and I've never forgotten it."

"You've got my undivided attention."

"Okay." She paused for dramatic effect. "There's a little man in your head."

"I know," I said. "He keeps telling me I was abducted by aliens."

Angela shot me a dirty look. "You'll *get* that whipping," she threatened, then continued. "This little man looks just like you. He does all your shooting for you. All day long. Can you picture him?"

I closed my eyes. "Yes. Handsome little devil."

Angela ignored me and continued. "Here's the key. He never misses. Understand?"

"Yes."

"Picture the ball going through the hoop every time." I did as I was told. "This guy's better than Jordan."

"That's the conceptualization I told you about the other day. The third *C*. It's also called *image shooting*. I read a thesis once in kinesiology class. It said the mind can't tell the difference between practicing and visualizing."

"You mean I can lay around all day and think about shooting, and it's just as good as going to the gym?"

"In theory. But I wouldn't chance it."

"Too bad. I'm sure my little man wouldn't make me run laps."

Angela grinned wickedly. "I'm glad you mentioned that. Take five more before you leave."

During the trip home, I pictured my little man making shot after shot. He definitely had more get-up-and-go than I did. Although I was physically exhausted, I felt good in a strange sort of way. I'd trade it any day of the week for the numbing mental and emotional by-product of my ex-profession. Whereas the daily deadlines of the ad game left me drained, my new physical routine had a cleansing effect. Still, it didn't make it any easier to drag my sorry ass into the house.

Pam was waiting for me by the front door.

"I've been worried about you," she said. "There's something wrong with your cell phone."

"Oops," I said.

"What *oops*?"

Sheepishly, I said, "I forgot to tell you. After I left Dunbar, I threw my phone out the car window. It was symbolic, sort of a last gesture of defiance."

Pam's face softened and she even managed to look mildly amused. "This from the man whose idea of rebellion is refusing to use the nine-digit zip code. You know, you've been acting very strange lately. Should I be concerned?"

"Not yet. I'll let you know when it's time to panic. Hey, I'm really sorry. Why didn't you just call the gym? They have a phone."

"I wasn't thinking clearly."

"Is everything okay?"

"I think so. You got a call from Bigg Fizz."

My stomach did a quick flip-flop. "They didn't change their minds, did they?"

"The man wouldn't tell me anything. He just said call him." She handed me a note with a name and number.

Trying to stay calm, I punched in the number and

waited an eternity for somebody to pick up. Pam hovered close by, looking anxious.

"Bigg Fizz, it's the bubbles. How may I help you?"

"Trip Treadwell, please." What kind of schmuck name was that, anyway? I didn't like this guy already.

"I'll transfer you now."

After a series of clicks and beeps, another voice came on the line. "Treadwell."

My own voice sounded thin and reedy by comparison. "This is Alan Nichols. The winner of the Three-Point Challenge."

"Yes, Mr. Nichols," Treadwell said cheerfully. "Thank you for returning my call."

"Is there a problem?"

"Not at all. I just wanted to introduce myself. I've been assigned to your, er, account. You might say I'm your liaison, as it were."

As it were. Was he or wasn't he? At least he sounded friendly, so to speak.

"Great," I said.

"If you need anything, anything at all, I'm your man. My main concern is to make this a most positive experience for you and your family. We'll be overnighting an itinerary, along with your airline tickets, limo transfer, and voucher for deluxe room accommodations. If you have any questions, please don't hesitate to call. Let me give you my private line."

I jotted down the number.

"Remember," he said, "Treadwell has all the answers."

"Thank you. I'll keep in touch." All the answers, huh? Maybe he could shed some light on that chicken and egg thing.

"Well?" Pam asked. She was twisting one strand of blonde hair around and around her index finger.

"We have our own liaison."

"Just what I always wanted. Does he do windows?"

"I don't think he does much of anything. Did I get any other calls?"

"That TV reporter again."

"Screw her. Want to hear about my day?"

"Sure."

"Well, there's a little man in my head …"

Later, just before we fell asleep, Pam said, "So, tell me about Angela." Perfectly innocent. Or not. Women aren't the simple, face-value creatures we men are.

"She really knows her stuff," I answered. "Very talented, very tough, no bullshit."

"Is she married? Does she have kids? Why'd she move to Vegas?"

I shrugged. "Don't know."

"How can you not know?"

"Easy. I never asked."

"What do you two talk about all day?"

"Basketball. What do you think we talk about?"

"That's the difference between us. If it were me, I'd know her whole life story by now."

"It never came up."

"You have to ask."

"Pry, you mean."

"No, ask. Slip it into the conversation."

"Like, how was my follow-through on that shot? And, are you married, by the way? Like that?"

Pam shook her head. "You're impossible."

"Here's a thought. When we have her over for dinner, you ask. I'll observe."

"Fair enough. What kind of food does she like?"

"I didn't ask."

9

In my dream, I was at the New Orleans Superdome, surrounded by 50,000 screaming fans. The basketball in my hand was the size of a beach ball. The basket was easily a hundred yards away. I could barely make out the backboard. Suddenly, the official handed me a ringing telephone. My dream popped like an over-ripe soap bubble and I realized, through the leftover suds in my head, that the ringing came from our phone on the nightstand. For the zillionth time, I marveled at Pam's ability to sleep through anything this side of a seven-point earthquake. I glanced at the digital clock. It was 6:10. A call this early was either bad news or a wrong number. Hoping for the latter, I fumbled for the receiver.

"Hello," I muttered.

"Alan Nichols?"

"Speaking."

"Rudy Kowalski, Las Vegas *Post*. I was wondering if I could ask you a few questions."

It was that stinking press release. And I wasn't even working for the bastard who issued it any more. Fully awake now, starting to get steamed, I said, "It's awfully early for an interview, isn't it?"

"I'm on deadline and I was hoping to catch you before you left for work."

"The ComPost, huh? I hate you guys."

The Las Vegas *Post*, unofficial right-wing mouthpiece of the casino cartel, is arguably the worst daily newspaper in the country. From my retro liberal viewpoint, you can count on them to be on the wrong side of every issue. Gun control? Unconstitutional. More firepower, that's the answer. Women's reproductive rights? Sorry. Get government off the backs of business and into the bedroom, where it belongs. The environment? Jobs come first. Nuke the rainforests. Minorities? A bunch of whiners and slackers. How about a little personal responsibility for a change? Not only did the *Post* preach this simplistic slop in its editorials, it seeped, like an oil spill, onto the front page. Even I know that's the cardinal sin of journalism. (Right after spelling somebody's name wrong.) I read the *Post* out of self-defense. It's good to know what the enemy's thinking.

Kowalski was persistent. "I'll only take a few minutes of your time."

"Here's an idea," I said. "Why not eliminate the middleman and send your paper directly to the recyclers."

"Very funny. Listen, we're going to run this story with or without your cooperation. I just need some quotes."

"Make them up like you usually do," I said, banging the phone down. I was starting to enjoy hanging up on people. It must have made a helluva noise, because Pam awoke with a start.

"Take it easy," she said. "It's not made of iron."

"Sorry."

"Who called so early?"

"Some reporter from the *Post*. I told him to get a real job."

"Did that make you feel better?"

I thought for a second. "Yeah. It's the new me. I don't take crap from anybody. Except you, of course."

Pam smiled. "Of course."

"You know, the *Post* is gonna run that story regardless. Maybe you'd better tell our friends and relatives before they read about it in the paper."

"You think they can read?"

"Just in case."

Fully awake now, I puttered around the house until it was time to head to the gym. I was surprised how quickly I was adjusting to my new routine. Make breakfast, clean the kitchen, feed the dog, catch the highlights on ESPN, wash up, change into shorts and sneakers. My years as an honest wage earner were beginning to fade like that Superdome dream. I've long suspected that working in an office is an unnatural act, a form of social and cultural brainwashing. Vacations and four-day weekends provide the strongest clue. The first day back always seems like a month. Then the day-in day-out repetition grinds you down, like water carving out the Grand Canyon, and that zombie look returns. Before you know it, you've rejoined your little band of pod people, doing the master's bidding, no questions asked. At least not out loud.

Today being Friday, Pam was getting ready for her business-law class at Community College. Her goal is to someday open a bed and breakfast in a place with trees and grass and cool summer evenings. In other words, a place the exact opposite of Las Vegas. She was laying the groundwork one piece at a time and would soon have her associate's degree. Opening the shower door, I told her goodbye, getting an especially wet kiss mixed with herbal shampoo. It wasn't half-bad. As I wandered down the hall, I could hear Amy's voice on the phone behind her closed bedroom door. "So he goes, 'No way,' and I'm all, 'Dude, get a life,' so he goes, 'Bite me,' and I'm like …" All that money for school and not a real verb in sight.

It was a perfect Vegas morning, the kind we get once a decade whether we need it or not. Appropriately enough, the sky was electric blue, divided into almost identical halves by a jet contrail somewhere over Nellis. The mountains, usually hazy gray specters hovering in the distance, jumped out like bas-relief. I rolled down the windows and switched on the radio, hoping for something worth listening to. Other than sports talk, there isn't much that's geared toward my target demographic. Contemporary Hit Radio, which used to be called Top 40, plays mainly rap and alternative; Soft Rock is for women; Classic Rock is a non-stop Zep-fest; and Country is soul music for rednecks. I usually land on the oldies station by default. Today, the radio gods were smiling, and I was treated to the Isley Brother's "This Old Heart of Mine" from the very beginning. As I belted out the chorus in a voice that makes even Flash run for cover, it occurred to me that I hadn't felt this good in years. Even when a little red Geo Metro darted out in front of me, so close I could read the "Mean People Suck" bumper sticker without squinting, I didn't launch into my usual profanity-laced tirade. I simply waved reflexively in answer to the "I'm sorry" gesture from the teenage girl behind the wheel. Pam might be right, I thought. Maybe it *was* time to panic.

After the now-familiar stretching exercises and short warm-up shots, Angela moved me all the way back to the free throw line.

"Just like the big kids," I said.

"It's time you developed some real skills," Angela replied. "Shoot a hundred."

My first attempt was an air ball. So was the second. The third caromed off the back iron all the way to where I was standing.

"Okay," Angela said, "make your adjustments."

I did. *Swish.* It was getting to be one of my favorite sounds.

"Put some more leg into it," Angela instructed. "You're pushing your shot."

After the first hundred, I was just under fifty percent. Not terrible, but nowhere near good enough. Angela wanted me at seventy-five percent before moving to the three-point line. "You need to work on a routine," she said.

"You mean like Rodney Dangerfield?"

"Nick," she said, "I swear I have no earthly idea what you're talking about half the time."

"Don't feel bad. Neither does anybody else."

"I bet you got beat up a lot when you were a kid."

"Not as much as you think. I was sneaky fast."

"Listen to me. I'm talking about a free-throw ritual. Some guys bounce the ball a couple of times, some spin it, some flex it over their heads. Karl Malone says a little prayer."

"I always wondered about that. How do you know?"

"My friend Leondra back home reads lips."

"I think God's probably tired of hearing from Karl by now. Whatever happened to saving it for the important things?"

Angela caught me off guard, saying softly, "I pray all the time."

"Really? How much could you possibly want?"

"Usually, it's just to say 'thank you.'"

I could feel my face turn bright red. "Okay, you're obviously an enlightened being, and I'm a first-class jerk."

"Good," Angela said. "Now that we both know our place, let's quit jawin' and get back to work. I don't care what moves you decide on, as long as it feels comfortable. Do the exact same thing each time. It'll program your brain. Lord knows it could use some programming."

I experimented with a variety of routines, including an Art Carney tribute that went on entirely too long. Just about the time Angela was getting ready to quit for good, I settled on a basic two-bounce approach. The ball banked through the hoop.

"You didn't call *glass*," Angela said. "Take five laps."

We worked on free throws the rest of the afternoon.

By the time we were done, I had improved to sixty-two percent, better than dozens of NBA players. Of course, I wasn't running up and down the court, dribbling, jumping, and getting elbowed in the nose every so often.

As we were getting ready to leave, Angela said, "Good practice today."

"Thanks. I thought so too. You're a great coach."

She smiled. "Well, I'm enjoying myself. Most of the time, anyway. You're a real piece of work, you know that?"

"It's part of my charm. Hey, I almost forgot. My wife Pam wants to meet you. She'd like you to come over for dinner some night."

"What about you?"

"Nah, we spend enough time together as it is."

"That's for sure."

"So, how about Sunday afternoon, say around five?"

"How can I resist an invitation like that?"

"Good. What kind of food do you like?"

"You know, Italian, barbecue, Southern. Anything but liver."

"Too bad. Pam was going to make her famous liver loaf. It's an old family recipe."

"I'm starting to figure you out. That's supposed to be funny, right?"

"More or less."

"One time I spent a weekend in L.A.," Angela said, "and I got a free ticket to sit in the audience of one of those game shows. They had signs all over the place to tell you when to applaud and when to laugh. I think you could use some of those."

I just smiled.

"So how about if we stick to barbecue?"

"I'll fire up the grill."

I followed Angela out to her car so she could jot down directions to my house. She drove a big blue Olds 98 that was aging worse than I was. The paint had oxidized, giving it a streaky multi-tone look, and rust had begun to creep up from the wheel wells. I noticed it still had Michigan plates.

"This is my hooptie, the official car of Detroit," she said. "It doesn't look like much, but at least it runs."

"What the hell's a hoop-dee?" I asked.

"That's what black folk call a beat-up run-down piece of junk like this." She patted its side tenderly. "Sorry baby, you know I don't mean it."

"Did you say 'black folk'? I thought you wanted to be called 'African Americans'."

She dismissed the question with a wave of her hand. "Personally, I don't care. I think we change it every few years, just to keep you white people guessing."

"It's working."

"Good. I don't get much feedback from the Caucasian community."

"You know, I've always thought that if I was a black man in this country, I'd be pissed off all the time," I said.

Angela gave me a curious look. "Why do you say that?"

"Because I'm a *white* man, and I'm pissed off all the time."

"What about?"

"You name it. Politics, society, hypocrisy, big business, bad drivers, over-priced pizza, people in general. It's all bullshit."

"The way I figure, everybody's got their cross to bear. Some are just draggin' around heavier ones, that's all. Yours ain't all that heavy, by the way." She yanked on the car door and it swung open with a loud groan.

My cheeks flushed again. "I know. Logically, anyway. But that doesn't make it any easier when some mouth-breather at the DMV sends me to the end of another line."

"It's all about focus, Nick. It's fine to be angry, but you gotta make it work *for* you, not against you. Same as in basketball. Let's say you get fouled hard going to the hoop and you're mad. Real mad. All you can think of is getting even, when you should be thinking about your game. Now you're out of control, not playing within yourself. As soon as that happens, the other guy wins."

"How'd you get so smart?" I asked.

"Not smart, just lucky. I come from a real close-knit family. They were always telling me about life, whether I wanted to hear it or not. Of course, when I was younger, I thought they were full of shit. But they wised up in a hurry."

"Funny how that happens. My daughter thinks I'm full of shit."

Angela chuckled as she slid onto the front seat. "Well, in your case, she might be right."

10

I stopped at McDonald's on the way home. Normally, I try to avoid the fast food joints, because the quality is a notch lower than your average high-school cafeteria lunch. But I needed something to fill me up in a hurry. Becoming a full-time jock had jump-started my metabolism and I found myself in need of refueling every couple of hours. Despite my increased consumption, the weight was falling off me. Before long, I would no doubt regain my boyish figure. Now, if I could just do something about my hair.

Although the place was practically empty, I had the misfortune of getting stuck behind an elderly woman and her mother. Apparently, the old lady was the only person in America who had never stepped foot in a McDonald's. "What do you put on that Big Mac?" she asked, as my stomach made urgent pleading sounds. Swell. Australian Aborigines can be heard singing, "Two all beef patties, special sauce, lettuce, cheese, pickles, onions on a sesame seed bun," on their walkabouts, and I'm waiting for Granny to get with the program. The counter girl, who looked like she got paid in Big Macs, had to recite the well-known list of ingredients twice because the older woman was also hard of hearing. They finally ordered, taking forever to pay with small change, and then it was my turn.

"I'm so old, I remember when McDonald's was fast," I said good-naturedly.

Ignoring my comment, she asked, "What's with the basketball?"

"Oh, this," I said. "It helps me focus."

She stared at me for a second before saying, "May I take your order please?"

"Just a Quarter Pounder and a medium iced tea," I said.

"Did you want fries with that?" she asked.

"No thank you."

"It's only ten cents more with the Meal Deal."

Impatience rising, I focused harder and just shook my head.

"They're really good."

"I know they are. They're famously good. But I just want a snack until dinner."

"Would you like to Super Size your drink?"

"I realize you're just doing your job," I said, "but please take my money and put in my order. If I don't get some food soon, I'm going to drop dead right here, and that's gotta be bad for business."

"Do you want to speak to my supervisor?"

"Only if your supervisor will feed me," I said a little too loudly, my focus going all blurry.

"I'll go get her."

"Please, don't," I begged. "Just take pity on me and give me my food."

"That'll be four eighty-five."

"Thank you, thank you," I said, practically sobbing. I handed her a twenty.

She gave me my change. "It'll be a few minutes. We don't pre-cook the Quarter Pounders this time of day."

I could have had a screaming fit right there and spent the night in jail, where the service was probably better. Instead, as soon as she turned her back, I left my twenty on the counter and snuck out the door. When the coast was clear, I made a dash for the adjacent convenience store, where I grabbed the giant economy sized Beer Nuts, a package of beef jerky, and a can of that iced tea that tastes like battery acid. I didn't care. It was food. I sat in the car and inhaled it, fortunate not to choke to death.

By the time I got home, my raging hunger headache had subsided. I stopped at the mailbox to retrieve the day's treasures. Getting the mail is one of the things that seemed more important when I was a kid. Along with April Fool's Day, the new TV season, and how the Dodgers are doing. But my advertising brain hadn't fully quit yet, so I went through it with a clinical interest.

The mail was the usual assortment of instant trash. Three offers to refinance my home, two pre-approved credit card applications (at 19.9 percent and 21.9 percent respectively), a pitch from another long-distance company I'd never heard of, an herbal cure for nighttime incontinence, and a *Time* magazine renewal notice. My subscription wouldn't be up for five months, but *Time's* concerned circulation department didn't want me to miss even one exciting issue.

I was about to dump the entire sorry lot when it occurred to me that I should have received my final paycheck by now. I shuffled through the envelopes again. Nothing with the distinctive red Dunbar and Associates logo. The check, when it came, would be better than a punch in the nose, but not much to show for twelve years of my life. Still, it would keep the wolf from the door for the time being. (Although there might be some coyotes lurking out by the curb.) I made a mental note to call Ginger, Joe Dunbar's gal Friday, if my money didn't arrive by early next week. Ginger knows where all the bodies are buried. That's because she buried most of them herself.

My thoughts were interrupted by the telephone. It was Pam, telling me she had a late meeting at our neighborhood homeowner's association, the good people who save us from the ravages of individuality. As Amy says, "They've got *way* too much time on their hands." I've often thought they should be called the Chicken Little Association, because no problem is too small for them to overreact to. Whether it's a mailbox that needs painting, or lawn grass an eighth of an inch too high, or teenagers cooking up the Ebola virus in mom's kitchen, the Association is on it with a vengeance, issuing warnings and handing out fines like a White House Special Prosecutor. In our case, I hadn't been bringing in the trashcan in a timely manner, and Pam was representing our interests. I suggested she plead insanity.

The point of her call was that Amy was out with friends, so I was on my own for dinner. Not a problem. When it comes to food, I'm the least picky person I know. Although I appreciate a gourmet meal as much as the next guy, quantity wins out over quality every time.

As soon as my snack wore off, I made myself a fine meal of Campbell's tomato soup and grilled cheese sandwiches. "Comfort foods," Pam calls them. Flash wandered over and I tossed him a small piece, which bounced off his snout. His timing had been off lately. He picked his prize off the floor and carried it protectively to the living room, where he licked it to a pulpy mess before putting it out of its misery.

After dinner, I sat in my recliner, closed my eyes, and watched the little man in my head reel off a couple hundred consecutive free throws. Angela was right. The guy couldn't miss. I wondered if he was eligible for the NBA draft. Around 7:45, just as I was nodding off, Pam came home.

"How's my favorite athlete?" she asked.

"Resting comfortably and able to take nourishment."

"Good."

"How'd it go at the inquisition? I don't see any burn marks."

"I got our penalty reduced from death to a twenty-five-dollar fine."

"I hope you wrote them a hot check."

"It's a little warm. But please promise you won't let the trash can stay out for weeks at a time."

"I feel like painting it day-glo orange and mounting it on the roof."

"Nick!"

"Okay, okay. Hey, before I forget, we're having company for dinner on Sunday."

Pam looked excited. "Angela?"

"The one and only. I'll pick up some steaks while I'm out tomorrow."

"You can do it on the way back from the mall."

"The mall?" The mall, any mall, with its artificial lighting, and mood-altering Muzak, and hoards of mindless shoppers, always makes me dizzy. Since finding out about catalogs and on-line shopping, I haven't ventured into one in years. "What about the mall?"

"Amy wants to take you for gym clothes."

"What's wrong with the ones I've got?"

"If you're going to be on television, you can't wear those crummy old shorts."

"Forget it," I said, knowing I'd already lost.

"Come on, it'll be fun. You and Amy can bond."

"No fair playing the bonding card. Besides, she's eighteen. All the bonding that's *gonna* be done *has* been done."

"Life isn't fair. You say that yourself."

"I give up. But call me on the cell phone after an hour and beam me the hell out of there."

She raised one eyebrow. "What cell phone?"

11

Saturday morning got off to a lousy start. For the second time in as many days, the phone woke me way too early. I waited for the answering machine to pick up, but it never did. Probably another power outage in the middle of the night. Vegas is famous for these, something else they never mention in the Chamber of Commerce brochures. The blinking numbers on the digital clock confirmed my suspicion.

"There oughta be a law," I grumbled, pulling the pillow over my head. After what seemed like the twenty-seventh ring, I grabbed it and snarled, "Somebody better be dead."

"Alan?" Only telemarketers and distant relatives call me Alan.

"Who wants to know?"

"It's me, Cousin Bill."

Bill, a second cousin on my mother's side, lives on the other end of town. In Vegas, that's like the other end of the world. Las Vegas Boulevard, a.k.a. the "Fabulous Strip," is a dividing line that separates the city into mirror images of strip malls, power centers and tract houses with Spanish tile roofs. It's a line that locals seldom cross, and then only with severe trepidation. On the few occasions I've wandered over to the west side, I found myself saying, "Thank God I don't live over here."

Bill and I have never been close. He only calls when he needs something. Being a semi-professional sports bettor, that something is usually money.

"What's the matter?" I asked. "All the other relatives get Caller ID?" Somewhere, I imagined Angela shaking her head in disappointment. But it was too early to focus. Besides, Bill is one of those people you just can't insult. Lord knows I've tried.

"You're a real kidder, you know that?" Bill wheezed. "Nah, I read about you in the paper and just wanted to say congratulations."

"Thanks. Why don't you call back later? Say, after sunrise." I hung up. Damn, the word was already out. Slipping into my robe, I stepped outside to get the *Post*. It may be a poor excuse for a newspaper but at least it comes early.

I plopped the paper on the kitchen table and spread it open. Sure enough, there on the front page of the Local section, just below the fold, was a file photo of me. I recognized it right away, along with the credit, "Photo courtesy of Dunbar and Associates." The headline read, "Local Man Already a Winner." The subhead explained, "Bottle Cap Worth Up to $1 Million."

With morbid curiosity, I continued.

"In a town built on games of chance, Alan Nichols may be the unlikeliest winner of all. Nichols, 43, an ex-advertising executive, recently became the recipient of the winning bottle cap in the national 'Bigg Fizz Million Dollar Challenge.' On March 23, Nichols will shoot a basketball from three-point range during halftime of the NCAA Western Region Finals in Phoenix, Arizona. If he makes the shot, he'll walk away with a cool million. Should he miss, the consolation prize is $50,000. Nichols, who could not be reached for comment, resigned his longtime position at Dunbar and Associates, a leading Las Vegas advertising firm, to devote all of his energy to basketball."

The story went on to quote some former business associates, including Jason McBride, ending with a statement from one Trip Treadwell, OmniCorp spokesperson, who said, "We're looking forward to seeing Mr. Nichols and his family in Phoenix, and wish him continued good luck in his quest for the million dollar prize." All in all, the article was better than I expected. Still, the genie was out of the bottle. Like a piece of candy on the kitchen floor, it would have all manner of vermin crawling out of the woodwork in no time.

Suddenly, I became aware of a familiar presence peering over my shoulder.

"Guess who?"

"Ashley Judd?"

"You always say that. You're no fun."

"That's not what it says in the *Post*. See, I'm famous."

Pam stared at the paper for a second. "Nice picture."

"Courtesy of good ol' Dunbar and Associates, still trading on my mug. Hey, did you hear who called this morning?"

"No, who?"

"Cousin Bill. He wanted to offer his heartiest congratulations. I hung up before he could ask for an advance on my winnings."

"Doesn't he owe us already?"

"Yep. He's a satisfied customer of Nick's National Bank. No interest, no penalties, take forever to pay. Amy's been making some withdrawals, too."

"I'll have a talk with her. By the way, don't forget you two are going to the mall today."

I made a face. "Don't I have a dentist's appointment or something?"

"Sorry. Can't you try to have a good time, just this once?"

"Sure. I can fake anything for an hour. Like sex."

Pam's eyes narrowed. "Since when does it last an hour?"

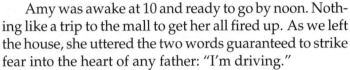

Amy was awake at 10 and ready to go by noon. Nothing like a trip to the mall to get her all fired up. As we left the house, she uttered the two words guaranteed to strike fear into the heart of any father: "I'm driving."

If Amy isn't the worst driver in Las Vegas, a city known for bad drivers, then she's a close second. Too close—as in right on the other guy's ass. At twenty miles over the speed limit, she believes in leaving exactly half a length between her and the car in front. No margin for error whatsoever. If the other guy should step on his brakes for any reason, let's say to avoid a dog or fake out a cop or cash in on a quick rear-end collision, Amy's Honda Civic would be a permanent trunk ornament. Driving conditions don't faze her. Rain, fog, solar eclipse, nothing keeps her from pushing that poor car to the limit. Pam and I have stayed up many a night, terrified, praying that she would come home in one piece, just so we could kill her ourselves. To our way of thinking, it's a miracle every time she walks in the door.

On this particular Saturday, I didn't feel like a confrontation, so I quietly opened the passenger door and buckled up, grateful that her car has dual air bags. Amy cranked up the radio and peeled out of the driveway without even a glance at the mirror. *Don't say anything*, I thought. If you live through this, you can make a donation to your favorite charity later.

"So," I asked, "which mall are we going to?"

"Las Vegas Factory Outlet. They've got the best deals."

"Isn't that kind of far?"

"Not for me." She hung a hard right and gunned us onto the I-15. I was thankful I'd eaten a light breakfast.

"Would you mind turning that music down a little?" I asked. "I can't hear myself think." The bass was jarring my fillings loose.

"No problem."

"What are we listening to, anyway?"

"Oldies station."

It didn't sound like any kind of oldies I was familiar with. "Who's the group?"

"The Offspring. They're from, like, 1998."

I tried listening for a few seconds. "What's that line mean, 'Pretty fly for a white guy?'"

"It means he's white, but he's cool."

"Like me?" I joked.

"Yeah. What*ever*."

There are two Amy's. The sullen belligerent Amy who surfaces when she's been deprived of food, sleep, or any of a hundred other creature comforts. That's the Amy we usually get. Or the pleasant sociable Amy who makes an appearance every four years, like the Olympics. I was indeed fortunate to be sitting next to that Amy this afternoon. In between swearing at the other drivers, ("Can you believe that asshole? Don't even think about it!"), she chattered on happily about school, work, boys, clothes, music, movies, and other assorted random neural misfirings, with just an occasional "Uh, huh" from me to keep her going.

Before I knew it, we were on the south end of the Strip at the Las Vegas Factory Outlet Mall, one of the eight shopping wonders of the world. A long line of tour buses waited patiently by the main entrance, disgorging passengers from as far away as Europe and Asia. More suckers pumping wads of cash into the local economy. If it kept them out of the casinos for even an afternoon, they were ahead of the game. At least they'd have something to show for their money.

Amy swung into a too-tight parking spot. I squeezed out of the car, pausing briefly to assess any damage, and we were off on our shopping adventure.

The Outlet Mall is roughly the same size as the Pentagon, only more dangerous. At any moment, for no apparent reason, a rubbernecking tourist can come to a complete stop in front of you, causing you to swerve wildly to avoid an ugly collision. It's like being trapped in some surreal video game where you don't know the rules. I felt fortunate to have Amy as my tour guide, steering me safely through the mall's many perils while keeping up a running commentary on the surrounding craziness. "Look at those ugly-ass shoes. What was she thinking? That woman shouldn't be wearing pants like that. Didn't she look in the mirror before she left the house? Oh my God, who told that chick she knew how to accessorize? Hel-lo. We're talking major fashion faux pas here. You can always tell the Euros by those stupid bowl haircuts. They don't smell so great, either. Lady, put your arms down, that's some crop you're growing there. Check out that couple. I'm *so* not into PDA. Hey, get a room!" And so it went, an endless stream of play-by-play. I had to admit I was having fun.

Our journey continued, past the identical clothing stores and kitchen gadget shops and knock-off perfume boutiques. Past the food court, with its Panda Express and Sbarro Pizza and Hot Dog On-a-Stick, whose hideous red, yellow and blue striped uniforms would make even Ashley Judd look like a clown. As we walked, I noticed boys checking Amy out, but she pretended to be oblivious. A good thing, too, because to my trained fatherly eye, they all looked like serial killers. As a young girl, Amy was always on the chubby side. Within the last few years, however, she had lost her baby fat and really come into her own. Of course, getting her braces off helped, too. I had about ten grand invested in her mouth, which was the main reason I always told her to smile.

"Are we there yet?" I asked, not exactly sure where "there" was.

"Twenty more minutes," Amy said mockingly, repeating the stock answer I always gave when she was a little girl, just as we embarked on our family vacation.

"I can't take another step," I said. "Go on without me and save yourself. Just leave me the gun."

She rolled her eyes. "Dad, you've got serious issues. Anyway, you can relax. We're here."

I looked up to see one of the most recognizable corporate logos in all of marketing, the Swoosh. We had arrived at our destination, the Mecca of the Mall, the Nike Store.

"I hate Nike."

"Chill, Dad. Nike's the bomb."

"That's a good thing?"

"And you thought you were fly."

"Can't we go someplace else? Doesn't Keds have an outlet?"

Amy rolled her eyes again. "Like they say on TV, 'Just Do It.'"

"You're a pod person," I said. "Doesn't it bother you that some third-world kids are making forty cents a week just so you can look good?"

"Actually, for them that's a good wage. It's either that or child prostitution."

"What are they teaching you at that college, anyway?"

"Come on, let's check out the sale racks. I'm all about the deals."

She took my hand and we entered the dreaded Nike store. Realizing that lightning was not going to strike me dead, at least not that very second, I loosened up just a little. Like the professional she was, Amy expertly led me through the maze of warm-up jackets and gym bags and shoes, until we arrived at an aircraft-hangar-sized area that housed the shorts and shirts.

"That's quite a selection," I said, feeling overwhelmed and slightly disoriented.

"Dad, you don't get out much, do you?"

"Until a week ago, all I ever did was work, remember?"

"I never gave it much thought."

That was true. In all her eighteen years, not once had Amy asked me about my job or even a simple, "How was your day?" On the one hand, I was happy she felt secure enough not to worry about mundane issues like where the money was coming from. On the other hand, nobody wants to be taken for granted, not even dads. I only questioned her about it once. She said, "I don't like it when you and Mom give me the third degree, so I try not to do it to you."

"Give me an example of the third degree," I said.

"Like when you ask 'How was school today?' Or 'What time will you be home?'"

"Don't you think, as your parents, we have a need to know?" I asked, baffled.

"You probably did when I was a kid, like fifteen or sixteen. But I'm all grown up now, Dad."

That led to a spirited (as in *loud*) discussion about rights and privileges and responsibilities. When it was over, much like the Israelis and Palestinians, nobody had budged an inch. From that point on, we settled into an uneasy truce and I counted the days until we would become empty-nesters. Ultimately, Amy would get married and have children of her own, and revenge would be mine.

But today, being a good little consumer was the only thing on her mind. She grabbed a pair of black shorts and a matching shirt. "These are stylin'," she said.

"They're a little long, aren't they?"

"Welcome to the twenty-first century."

"All right, let's buy them and get out of here."

"Dad, you're hopeless. You need more than one outfit."

"What for?"

"What if they interview you? You can't be wearing the same thing every time."

"Why not?"

"You wouldn't understand. It's just the way it is, okay?"

"Fine. How about these green shorts?"

"Yuck. What is it with you and green?"

"I like green."

"It's like the worst color ever."

"I give up. Get whatever you want."

With a determined look, Amy deftly maneuvered through the rows of clothing, picking out gear in gold, red, and some sort of plaid. It might be good for washing the car, I noted, if I ever ran out of rags. Amy took great pains to point out the size and placement of the Nike logo on each garment. For some reason, this was important. As far as I was concerned, Nike should pay *me* for being their walking billboard.

"There," she said, admiring her handiwork. "You're hooked up. Now all you need is some socks."

"I have plenty of socks."

Amy made a face. "*Tube* socks." She spit out the words in disgust. "Nobody wears tube socks."

"What do they wear, I hesitate to ask?"

"These," she said triumphantly. "Ankle socks." She held them up for me to examine. They were tiny. In this brave new world, shorts were longer and socks were shorter.

"*Guys* wear these?"

"Of course."

"When I was a kid, socks like these would've gotten me killed."

"Sure, but things were different back around the Civil War. Do you want my help or not?"

"You know I do."

"Then deal with it."

"Whatever you say. Did you bring your Visa card?"

"Yeah right! You're lucky I'm not charging a consulting fee."

"Tell you what. I'll buy you a frozen yogurt on the way out."

The bill, not counting tax and yogurt, was a hundred eighty-five dollars and change. For gym clothes. On sale at the outlet mall. I'm always shocked by how much things cost. To me, major purchases, like a house or a car, should be about a thousand bucks, and everything else should be less than ten.

"Did you two have fun?" Pam asked when we got home.

"Oodles," I said.

"Show me what you bought."

Amy excitedly opened the bag and held up each item, one by one, as if they were priceless artifacts.

"Very nice," Pam said.

"Really?" I asked.

"Sure. You guys did great."

"Try them on," Amy urged. "Let's see those bad boys."

Despite my protests, I wound up putting on an impromptu fashion show, pretending to be the smiling wrinkle-free man in the Sears catalog, one arm akimbo, the other outstretched, shaking hands with nobody. I elicited oohs and aahs and the occasional catcall from the admiring crowd.

"I still think these are too long," I said of the shorts. "They go way past my knees."

"You'll get used to them," Amy assured me. "But look at those legs. They're so white. Why don't you mix in a trip to the tanning salon?"

"That'll be the day," I said. I've never understood the concept of tanning salons in the desert, places for people who want to kick their melanomas into overdrive.

"So," I said when I had tried on my last article of clothing, "did anybody call?"

"Just everybody," Pam said. "Friends, relatives, reporters, salespeople, three guys who claim to be your long lost brother, and the Divine Something Church. For a $500 tax deductible donation, they'll put in a good word for you with the Big Guy."

"Shaq?"

"They didn't say."

"Don't these people take a day off?"

"Oh, and Jason called," she said.

"I told him maybe we'd get together this weekend."

"I invited him to join us for dinner on Sunday."

"As usual, I bow to your impeccable hostess instincts."

"You may arise. Did you remember the steaks?"

"What do you think?"

"I think you'd better get your butt over to the supermarket."

12

The doorbell rang on Sunday at exactly 5 pm.

"I'll get it," I yelled when I realized nobody else was bothering.

It was Angela. She wore a flowery bright yellow dress and carried a bottle of wine and a videotape.

"Come on in," I said. "You're right on time, as usual."

"It's a bad habit I picked up from my nursing days. Here, I brought you a little somethin' somethin'." She handed me the gifts.

"Thanks. What's with the video? Porn, I hope."

"Pacers vs. Knicks, 1995 Eastern semis."

"And this is important because …"

"Reggie Miller, only the best pure shooter in the league. Watch the fourth quarter every night before you go to bed."

"You're always working, huh?"

"Gotta earn that thousand bones a week you're payin' me."

"You look nice, by the way. I don't think I've ever seen you in clothes before."

Angela smiled. "Don't say that too loud. I wouldn't want your wife to get the wrong idea."

Pam appeared suddenly from the kitchen. "I don't worry about Nick," she said. "If he ever fooled around, her name would have to be Pam, or he'd mess up big time."

"Angela, I'd like to introduce you to my housekeeper, Cruella."

"Stop it," Pam ordered, brushing past me. She gave Angela a warm hug. "I'm Pam, Nick's better half."

"Angela Jackson. Thanks for inviting me. I don't get a home-cooked meal very often, unless I cook it myself."

"Well, with Nick working the grill, it's fifty-fifty. You might have to reset your mouth for pizza."

"A word to the wise; always be nice to the chef," I said. "I'll go check the coals, so you kids can trash me in private. Angela, how do you like your steak?"

"Rare."

Pam scrunched up her face. "So does Nick. I think I'll put you both at the far end of the table."

As I left for the back yard, I heard Angela say, "What can I help with?"

"Not a thing," Pam said. "Just keep me company. Let's crack that bottle of wine."

While I fiddled with the grill, I could hear Pam and Angela's conversation drifting through the open kitchen window. Their voices were musical, like human wind chimes, one alto, one soprano, punctuated by giggles and the occasional burst of laughter. Funny how women can become instant best friends, while men rarely move beyond sports, cars, and babes. I like our way better. Less messy.

"I'm so glad we finally met," Pam said. "Nick speaks very highly of you."

"I'll bet."

"No, really. He says it was fate you two got together. And, trust me, Nick doesn't believe in fate, or anything else for that matter."

"He's different, I'll give you that."

"He grows on you."

"Like a wart?" Laughter. The sisterhood was in full bloom, at my expense.

"So," Pam said, "be honest. Does he have a snowball's chance of making this shot?"

"Sure. My Aunt says even a stopped clock is right twice a day."

"Seriously."

"He's doing good for a man with limited skills. I don't think he'll embarrass himself. And who knows, the ball might even go in. Stranger things have happened."

"I'm trying not to get my hopes up."

"That's probably wise."

"Nick tells me you used to play in college."

"Yeah, I was pretty decent, if I do say so myself. Then I ripped up my knee and decided to go to nursing school."

"What brought you to Vegas, of all places?"

"Take one guess."

"A man."

"Yep. Same old story. You'd think we'd learn by now."

"Not a chance. What happened?"

"I met Clyde at Henry Ford Hospital in Detroit …"

"Wait a minute," Pam interrupted. "His name's Clyde?"

"Uh-huh."

"Well, that should've been your first clue. Guys named Clyde are always bad news."

"Tell me about it. Next time, I want somebody with a normal name like Deion or Hakeem or 50 Cent. Anyway, they brought Clyde in for an emergency appendectomy. I was his nurse on the day shift. First time I ever got involved with a patient. Last time, too. Girlfriend, that man could charm the spots off a leopard. And he recovered in a hurry, if you know what I mean. We went out for a few months, pretty serious I thought, and then he dropped the bomb. Told me he got a job as a dealer in Vegas, did I want to come? I thought it over, decided to go for it, and here I am."

"And where's Clyde?"

"Don't know, don't care. His job fell through, then he started drinkin' and gamblin' and losin' his money. Then stuff of mine started disappearing. Money, jewelry, you name it. One day he asks me, real casual, if I have the pink slip to my car. That's when I knew I'd better get out of there, or I'd be walking to work."

"And then you lost your job."

"Ain't that a bitch. I gotta say, this town knows how to kick you when you're down. I'd be back in Detroit by now if I hadn't run into Nick."

"Well, I'm glad you did. More wine?"

"Sure. So how'd you and Nick hook up?"

"Would you believe a blind date?" Pam said.

"No way. Those never work out."

"Well, this one did. We were both living in L.A. Nick sold advertising for one of the local cable TV stations. He's five years older than me. He claims he raised me, but don't believe it. I was always more mature. Anyway, a big client of his kept bugging him about this girl he knew, the daughter of an old family friend. That was me. The client thought we'd be perfect for each other. Nick managed to duck him for months, until the guy threatened to pull his account. So he finally called. That's my Nick, an incurable romantic. I had just gotten a puppy, and when Nick came to the door, I was cleaning puppy puke off my blouse. Didn't even faze him. We went out for a nice seafood dinner, then hung around some old jazz club he liked. I thought he was funny and cute. After we got back to my place, we stayed up all night laughing."

"That's *all* you did?"

"Honest. He didn't make his move until our next date."

"I never knew a man like that."

"Neither did I. I figured he was a real gentleman. Or gay."

Mercifully, the conversation was cut short by the doorbell. After a few moments, Pam appeared in the back yard, followed by Jason McBride.

"Look who's here," Pam said.

"Boy, am I glad to see you," I told Jason. "These women have me severely outnumbered. Did you know I'm the only guy in this household? Even my dog is neutered."

I handed him a beer.

"So, how's retirement treating you?" Jason asked after Pam went back inside.

"I wouldn't know. I'm working harder than ever, down at the gym from dawn 'til dusk, practicing. I have a coach and everything."

"I know, Pam just introduced us. I think it's great."

"Good, because I gave her your ten percent."

"No big deal. I'll just have to kick your ass." Jason checks in at about six-two and weighs about a buck ninety-five.

"Think you can take me? I'm pretty pumped. Look, a muscle," I said, flexing my poor excuse for a bicep.

"I'm impressed. So, you want the office gossip or not?"

"Absolutely not."

"Briggs, Fletcher, and Riley are all fighting for your old job."

I put my hands over my ears. "I can't hear you."

"The old man made them all submit resumes and reapply."

Reluctantly, I put my hands down. "He did? What a player."

"And here's the best part. All three of them have to do a marketing plan and spec campaign for one of our new clients. Talk about getting free work. How funny is that?"

"I have to admit. Dunbar's really got them squirming, huh?"

"Yeah. And when it's all over, he'll probably bring in some hired gun from outside the agency."

I smiled with bitter satisfaction. "Fuck 'em all. They deserve each other."

"You don't miss all the bullshit?"

"Not one bit."

"Well, I can't say I blame you." He took a swig of beer for emphasis. "There's been some other weird stuff going on, too. Dunbar's been huddled up behind closed doors with a bunch of corporate types. Nobody knows what the hell's going on. But that doesn't stop the rumors from flying."

"Like what?" My level of interest surprised me.

"Either we're getting ready to merge with another firm or Dunbar's wife is filing for divorce. Those are the top two, as far as I can tell. Maybe I should start an office pool and pick up some quick cash."

"Now you're talking." I took a pull off my own beer.

"Anyway, I'm keeping my eyes open. I've been thinking about calling one of those headhunters."

"Just make sure they can keep a secret. You know how those ad guys like to yack. Dunbar'll find out about it before you get back to the office. Remind me, and I'll give you a name before you leave. Somebody you can trust."

"Thanks, Nick."

I glanced at my watch. "Shop talk is officially over."

"Well, then," Jason said, "I've been wondering. If you sink your shot, what are you gonna do with the money?"

"Not to worry. Pam's got it all worked out."

"I know what you mean." As a young single guy in Vegas with an actual job, Jason attracts women who have no problem spending his hard-earned cash. More than once, he's been known to complain, "Doesn't anybody know how to order something besides Dom Perignon?"

"To be honest, I'm trying not to think about it," I said. "Besides, it's not like I need anything."

"How about a new ride?"

"What's wrong with the Camry?" I asked in mock disbelief.

"Well, the least you could do is get it washed."

"And rinse away all those memories? That car's like a

moving archaeological dig. Nah, if I win the money, I'm gonna simplify my life. No to-do lists, no fax machines, no cell phones, no pagers, no voice mail, no e-mail, no Web sites. Have you noticed, everybody's got a fuckin' Web site. Even that homeless guy at Sahara and I-15. I hear he's franchising."

"Ground-floor opportunity," Jason said, grinning. Then, serious again, "But isn't there something you've dreamed about?"

"I just want to live long enough to see Britney Spears in Playboy."

"Could be any day now," Jason laughed. "I mean, besides that."

"I can't even remember. All I want is a comfortable home with a big porch, in the middle of nowhere. A mile from my nearest neighbor. No 7-Eleven stores on every corner. Maybe I'll ride a bike, won't even need a car. And every evening, around dusk, I'll sit on that big old porch with a cold one and thank my lucky stars I got the hell out of here."

"I know you, you'll be bored in a week."

"I doubt it. But give me a chance to find out."

From inside the house, Pam yelled, "How's the fire looking?"

"Perfect," I called back. "The coals are almost white."

"You'd better put the steaks on. We'll be ready in fifteen minutes."

"The master chef is on the case." I turned to Jason. "How do you like your steak?"

"Medium."

I took the smallest steak and tossed it on the grill, watching the flames leap up to greet the first arrival. This one was for Amy, who preferred hers charred past all recognition.

"So, how about you?" I asked Jason. "You might be coming into a nice chunk of change. What's on your agenda?"

"I'm not telling," he said, sounding like a five-year-old. "You'll just make fun of me."

"No, I won't. I promise."

"Well, the happiest time of my life was when I lived in Redondo Beach, in a little converted garage apartment on the Strand," he said, warming to his subject. "Me and my buds surfed all day, partied all night, picked up odd jobs when the money ran low. I've heard you can't go home again, but what if I invested in a surf shop or some rundown pizza place? I could make a few bucks and still get back to the beach. Pretty lame, huh?"

"I'm not laughing," I assured him. "If that's what you want, I say go for it. The worst thing you can have is regrets. Do it now, before you get saddled with a wife and kids." I threw a couple more steaks on the grill.

Jason fixed me with a penetrating stare. "That doesn't sound like the happily married guy I know."

"Don't get me wrong. I wouldn't trade my wife and daughter for anything in the world. All I'm saying is, get everything out of your system while you're young, because marriage has a way of side-tracking you. You work your ass off and when you finally look up, it's twenty years later."

"But now you've got a chance to get it all back," he said. "So tell me, are you gonna make this shot or what?"

"You'll have to ask my coach. All I know is, I'm improving."

"Gnarly, dude."

"I've never understood what that means."

"Who knows? I'm just brushing up on my surf talk."

Dinner couldn't have been more pleasant. The women polished off the wine, so Jason and I grabbed some more beers from the ice chest. The steaks were perfect, no complaints. Even Amy seemed to like hers. "It's grubbin'," she said. We all talked and laughed and enjoyed each other's company, as the food and alcohol combined to create one of those happy scenes normally reserved for Bigg Fizz commercials. We even managed to avoid talking about basketball. Then, somewhere between the last corn-on-the-cob and the first bite of dessert, the conversation took a detour.

"I can't believe everything that's happening around here," Amy said. "It's just so awesome." She turned to Angela. "I took my dad shopping for new gear yesterday. Wait'll you see him in it. I always tell him, you can't do your best unless you look your best."

I said, "It's the closest thing she has to a philosophy."

Amy rolled her eyes. "Okay, basketball boy, let's ask your coach. What do you think about what I said?"

Angela paused for a moment before saying, "I'm for anything that gives you an edge."

"See, Dad? I was right."

"But," Angela continued, "it all comes from inside. What your dad really needs is *attitude*."

"He's got lots of attitude," Amy said. "All bad."

Angela laughed. "I know, but that's not what I'm talkin' about. He's got to believe in himself, that the ball's gonna go through the hoop every time he puts it up."

Pam chimed in, "And how does he get this attitude?"

Angela didn't hesitate. "The same way we all do. Face the fear."

"What fear?" Amy asked.

"Whatever he's most afraid of. Only your dad can answer that for sure."

"I get it," Amy said. "It's like the time I had to give an oral report in my American Lit class. I was so nervous, I thought I was going to faint. But when it was over, I felt really good about myself."

"Exactly," Angela said.

Now everyone was staring at me while I squirmed

in my seat. Finally, Pam asked, "So, what is it, Nick? What scares you the most?"

"Right now, I'm scared of missing dessert," I tried weakly, in a futile attempt at changing the subject.

"Be serious, for once," Pam shot back.

"I don't know. The usual stuff. Spiders, snakes, heights, the Robinsons-May bill."

"Ha ha," Pam faked a laugh.

"But I'll be damned if I'm trying out for 'Fear Factor' just to develop some attitude. Couldn't I get a tattoo or something? All the NBA players have them now."

"Over my dead body," Pam said.

"Maybe a nice Superman logo, or a skull." I snapped my fingers. "I know. I'll get your name tattooed on my ass."

"I don't think your next wife will like that," Pam said.

"Never mind. It probably hurts like hell, anyway."

"No it doesn't," Amy blurted out.

We all looked at her.

"Or so I've heard," Amy said, suddenly interested in the leftovers on her plate.

"We'll talk to you later, young lady," Pam said.

"Well, then, if I can't have a tattoo, what about getting my ear pierced?"

"Dad, that's so not today for older men," Amy said. "Unless you're a pirate."

Pam agreed. "You might not want to call attention to those ears."

"Then I'll shave my head. It's not like I've got that much hair to begin with. It'll make me a badass, like those pro wrestlers."

Now it was time for Angela to put in her two cents worth. "Nick, white guys should never shave their heads."

"Why not?"

"It'll make you look like a giant thumb." She paused. "Or a penis."

That was more than my so-called family and friends could take. Mild amusement turned to waves of laughter. It built up, reached a crescendo, started to subside. Then somebody said "penis" again, and the whole cycle repeated itself. Before long, they were wiping tears from their eyes.

"I'm glad you're all having such a good time," I said. "I hope you wet yourselves."

When the snorts and guffaws died down, Jason, who'd been largely silent up to this point (except for the beer foam that came flying out of his nose), said, "Nick, you mentioned something about heights."

"Yeah, isn't that like a universal fear or something?"

"Sure is. How do you feel about sky diving?"

"I think it's a very bad idea."

"I agree," said Pam. "I can't even get Nick on a ladder to change the battery in the smoke alarm."

"I *like* that chirping noise," I protested.

"Well," Jason continued, "what about bungee jumping? They've got a really excellent one next to Circus Circus."

"No fucking way. Pardon my language."

"We've all heard it," Pam said disapprovingly.

"Amen," Angela chimed in.

Jason kept plugging away. "It's totally safe."

"Says who?"

"Have you ever heard about a bungee accident on the news?"

"No, but it's not like I've been paying attention."

"They've never had one problem."

"With my luck, I'd be the first. How do you know so much about it, anyway?"

Jason glanced around the table before saying quietly, "I've done it."

"You're kidding," I said.

"Cool," Amy said.

"More than once," Jason said. He poked around in

his wallet. "See, I have a punch card." He flashed the tattered card proudly. It had five holes in it. They looked like little coffins to me. "One more jump and I get a free-bie."

"Whoopee," I said. "How come you never told us at work? What are you, some kind of extreme guy?"

He shrugged. "I knew you'd all give me a hard time."

"Good call," I said.

"So, come on. Let's go this Saturday. It's the most in-credible rush. I can't even describe it."

"That's because you're brain damaged," I said. "From all the jumping."

"Pam, what do you think?" Jason asked. "Help me out here."

"Nick's a big boy. He always makes his own dumb decisions."

"Angela, say something," Jason said. "He'll listen to you."

Angela leaned back in her chair, pondering. At length, she said, "Well, you'd never get *me* up there, but I think it's a good idea. For Nick." She swiveled to look me in the eye. "See, if you can make yourself do this, you'll never be nervous about some basketball shot. Or any-thing else."

I gave her a dirty look. "Thanks, Coach. For noth-ing."

Jason's eyes glowed. He said, "So it's a done deal."

"I never said that," I told him. "Here's the best I can do. I'll go with you next weekend and check it out. If I like the looks of the place, maybe I'll give it a try."

"All right!"

"Way to go, Dad," Amy said. "Wait'll I tell my friends. Can I come and watch?"

"Sure," I said. "Invite the whole damned world while you're at it. We'll get a group rate."

"It'll be fun," Jason said.

"Fun," I repeated flatly. Already, my mind was feverishly cooking up excuses. If all else failed, maybe I'd get lucky and die between now and Saturday.

Just before bedtime, I plugged in Angela's tape and watched Reggie Miller single handedly plunge a dagger deep into the heart of the New York Knicks. Now *there's* a guy with attitude, I thought. I wondered how he felt about bungee jumping.

13

On Monday morning, I got to the gym early, even before Angela. I was feeling slightly apprehensive about the two-day layoff, how it would affect my shot. As I checked in at the front desk, the girl I had come to think of as "Heidi" smiled at me and said, "I saw your picture in the paper. Congratulations."

"Thank you."

"We had no idea who you were. We all just thought you were some jobless guy."

"Well, I'm that, too," I joked.

"Don't get me wrong," she said brightly. "I think you're a very attractive older man." Her jade green eyes sparkled.

Was she coming on to me? I was only about twenty years out of practice. Blushing, I managed to say, "I'm flattered. But I'm old enough to be your ... uncle."

She laughed, a sweet melodious sound. "Well, I know you've got work to do. We can talk more later."

"Okay."

"Can you do me one favor?"

"What's that?" I asked, briefly imagining all manner of fascinating propositions.

"When you're on TV, can you give a shout out to the Rec Center? That would be so cool. We could definitely use the pub."

"I'll do my best."

She smiled again and said, "Have a nice practice."

I had no idea what that conversation was all about, but I was sure of one thing. It would be hard to keep my mind on basketball. As I was going through my stretching routine, Angela showed up.

"Thanks again for dinner last night," she said. "I had a nice time. You've got a wonderful family."

"I just rent them for special occasions."

"Well, it made me homesick. In a good sort of way."

"I'm happy we could all get together. But I still don't know how I got suckered into bungee jumping."

"It'll put hair on your chest."

"That's not where I need it." Anxious to change the subject, I asked, "So what's on today's agenda?"

"I thought we'd start with free throws. If you look good, it's time to move you back to three-point range."

"I'm a little worried about the two days off. Like my daughter says, what if I suck?"

"You might be surprised."

I *was* surprised. Pleasantly. After a hundred shots from the charity stripe, I tallied an impressive seventy-nine percent. Even my misses were close. Most times, I could tell where the ball was going the instant it left my hand.

"You've got a nice rhythm going there," Angela said. "Sometimes a little break in the action is just what you need."

"I feel good," I said. "Just like James Brown."

"Okay, James, move to the top of the key."

I did as instructed, immediately noting the four-and-a-half-foot difference. From there, the basket seemed small and distant, like looking through the wrong end of a telescope. I felt my confidence drain away, leaving me shaken and stirred. "Here goes nothing," I thought, and I was right. My first shot hit the bottom of the net. Unfortunately, it never went through the top of it.

"It's like starting from scratch, isn't it?" Angela said.

"That's for sure. What now?"

"More leg, more arc. Shoot as hard as you can and see what happens."

What happened was, the ball hit the front of the rim. This was even tougher than it looked.

"You might need to visit the weight room, build up those legs," Angela suggested.

"Do we have time?"

"We'll make time."

Just then, I heard a ruckus out by the lobby. Looking over, I saw a well-dressed young woman enter the gym, followed by a slovenly man lugging a professional video camera. As they drew closer, I noticed a logo on the camcorder. *"Channel 8 Action News,"* done in one of those typestyles that make the letters look like they're moving very quickly. Behind our new guests, Heidi stood at the door, yelling, "Ma'am, you'll have to take off those high heels!" The woman stopped briefly, kicked off her shoes, and continued marching toward us.

"Shit, we're busted," I whispered to Angela.

"Who are they?"

"TV reporters. 60 Minutes wannabes. I guess it's too late to run."

"Probably."

"Well, let's play this by ear."

By now, the woman was upon us. She appeared to be in her late twenties, Hispanic-looking, attractive in a buttoned-down and made-up kind of way.

"Alan Nichols?" she asked.

"Who wants to know?"

"Jennifer Santiago, Channel Eight Action News."

"I'm sorry, Nichols had to leave suddenly. You just missed him."

The reporter tilted her head and gave me a quizzical look. "Mr. Nichols, I've seen your picture."

"Yeah. So how'd you find me?"

"Trade secret. It wasn't that tough. If I can just take a few moments of your time … "

"Okay. But make it fast. You're interrupting my life's work."

"Thank you," she said. Her smile was dazzling. "Mike, are you ready to roll?" she asked the cameraman.

"All set."

"Then we'll go in three, two, one. I'm standing in the East Las Vegas Recreation Center with Alan Nichols, winner of the Bigg Fizz Million Dollar Challenge. Mr. Nichols, what was your reaction when you learned you'd be shooting a three-pointer for a possible million-dollar prize?"

She stuck the microphone in my face. "The first thing that crossed my mind was, 'un-fucking-believable.'"

"Cut!"

"What's wrong?"

"Mr. Nichols, this is for broadcast television. You can't say words like that."

"But that was my reaction. You wouldn't want me to lie, would you?"

"Can't you just clean it up a bit?"

"Isn't that censorship? What about my First Amendment rights?"

"Please be cooperative," she begged. "I'm on deadline here."

"I'll try. We can't have you missing your deadline."

"Okay, take two, in three, two, one." She repeated her introduction and question, word for word. Then it was my turn again.

"My first thought was, 'unbelievable.' I never won anything before in my life."

Jennifer Santiago nodded. "Then what happened?"

"I quit my job and hired a full-time coach. Angela Jackson. She was a star in college." The camera panned over to Angela.

"Ms. Jackson, may I have a few words with you?"

Angela looked down and shuffled her feet before saying, "Sho'."

"How is Mr. Nichols doing? What are his chances of making the million-dollar shot?"

"He be doin' jes' fine fo' a white boy," Angela said. "Too bad he ain't no nigga, he be doin' even betta." She flashed an exaggerated goofy grin.

"Cut!"

"What now?" I asked.

"We can't air this."

"Why not?"

"It's so …" Jennifer Santiago fumbled for the word, before settling on "racial."

"That's the way she talks."

"Well, we'll just have to edit this back at the studio. Thank you for your trouble."

"No trouble at all," I said. "Any time."

The reporter and her flunky packed up their gear and tramped toward the exit, dejected. As soon as the coast was clear, I said to Angela, "Nice dialect."

"It *do* come in handy sometime."

With that, we laughed so hard, we could hardly stand up. It made the rest of the day even more fun than usual.

Unfortunately, Jennifer Santiago had the last laugh. That night, as Pam and I were getting ready for bed, Amy yelled from her room, "Quick, turn on Channel Eight! You're on the news!" I clicked on the TV just in time to catch a glimpse of myself saying, "… and hired a full-time coach." The camera cut to Angela, grinning but silent, followed by another shot of me, under Jennifer Santiago's serious announcer-school voice: "Alan Nichols has less than three weeks to prepare for his million-dollar chance of a lifetime. Whether he'll walk away a winner or loser remains to be seen. For now, only one thing is certain. He's hoping not to come up short." As she finished, the camera cut to a medium shot of me badly missing my first three-point attempt.

The happy-talk anchor back at the studio chuckled, "Looks like he's got his work cut out for him."

His airhead partner agreed.

"Damn, I didn't see them taping that shot. I'm gonna be a laughingstock." I turned to Pam, who looked like she was about to bust a gut herself.

"You have to admit, it's pretty funny," she said.

"I don't have to admit anything."

"Dad, you'd better practice more!" Amy yelled from down the hall.

"Another country heard from." I turned off the tube and crawled into bed. Pam made me forget all about Jennifer Santiago.

14

By now, I was a minor celebrity at the gym. "Good morning, Mr. Nichols," Heidi greeted me on Tuesday morning.

"Call me 'Nick,'" I suggested.

She smiled. "Okay, Mr. er … Nick. I saw you on the news last night."

"I didn't think young people watched the news," I said. Maybe she was stalking me. I could think of worse things.

"I was surfing through the channels and there you were. They weren't very nice to you."

"Never believe anything you see on TV."

"Anyway, we're sending a bill to the station. That woman reporter scratched up the gym floor with her heels."

"That's the best news I've heard in a long time." Final score: Nick two, reporter one.

As I turned to leave, Heidi said, "Maybe we could go for a cup of coffee sometime." I walked into the gym with an extra spring in my step.

I was going to need it. Angela threw me the ball.

"You're late," she said.

"Aw, two minutes."

"Let's get to work."

"Nice to see you, too. Tough night?"

"My ex-boyfriend Clyde caught my act on the news. I didn't even think he owned a TV. Probably saw it in some bar. He called me real late, said he wants to get back together. So much for keeping a low profile."

"What'd you tell him?"

"I said I'd think about it. Then, first thing this morning, I called the phone company and changed my number. I know Clyde. He smells a buck and wants in on it."

"Well, if you need a place to lie low for a while, we have an extra room."

"Thanks."

"Just let me know ahead of time, so I can move all the exercise equipment. The stationary bike is covered with hanging clothes."

"Are you gonna keep jawin' or are you gonna put the ball in the hole?"

"What do you think?"

"I think you'd better shoot a hundred from the three-point line, so I can see how much trouble we're in."

We were in considerable trouble. Twenty-seven-out-of-a-hundred trouble, to be exact.

Angela knew when to be encouraging and when to kick me in the ass. She sensed that the gentle approach was what I needed today.

"Don't get down on yourself," she said in soothing tones. "Just go back to your free-throw form, with a little something extra. If you have to, pretend it's a jump shot."

I jumped as high as I could, a full two inches off the floor, and watched as the ball sailed through the basket.

"That's more like it," I said. In the back of my mind, I could hear the crowd cheering enthusiastically.

Over the next couple of hours, my overall success rate improved, although I was still wildly inconsistent. I'd sink six or seven in a row, only to miss the next ten. Just as I began to think I had it wired, everything would fall apart. A metaphor for my life, if there ever was one. At last, I reached a point of diminishing returns, failing on my last fourteen attempts.

"That's enough for today," Angela said.

"Great. Nothing like ending on a positive note."

"How's your arm feel?"

"Like it belongs to somebody else."

"Go home, ice it for a half-hour. Then sit back, relax, and crank up the mental imagery. You'll do better tomorrow."

"Are you sure?"

"Trust me. That's why I've got TV reporters and ex-boyfriends hounding me."

As usual for this time of day, I returned to an empty house. Pulling out a chair, I parked myself at the kitchen table and flipped through the mail. Still no check. Son of a bitch! I flung the stack of envelopes at the trashcan, missing it completely. Flash stirred from his nap and arched an eyebrow, as if to say, "Keep it down, will ya?" Time to call Ginger and find out what the hell was going on. After taking a few moments to calm myself, I punched in her private number.

"Hi, Ging," I said in my friendliest tone. I was glad she couldn't see me pacing.

"Who is this?"

"It's me, Nick. How quick we forget."

"Oh, Nick."

"Nice to hear your voice, too. Hey, here's a question for you. Where's my check?"

I thought I heard an involuntary gulp. Or maybe it was just noise on the line. "Your check?"

"Yeah. I'm supposed to have it by now."

"Actually, that's not entirely true," Ginger said in her most officious manner. Whatever had spooked her, she regained her footing in a hurry. "By law, when a person resigns their position, we have until the next regularly

scheduled payday, or seven days, whichever comes first."
Ginger was always on solid ground when laying down
the law.

"It was a week yesterday," I said, feeling a little like
Perry Mason.

"Then I'm sure we mailed it out," Ginger said.

"Could you look into it for me, please?" I asked,
amazed at my composure. "Just to make sure it didn't
fall through the cracks." Then, for good measure, "I'd
hate to call the Labor Board on you."

"Technically, it's the Labor *Commission*," she said icily. "I'll give you the number, if you'd like. Ask for Mona."

"I'm sure that won't be necessary."

"You're right. I'll find out about your check."

"Thanks, Ging. You're a peach." *A big fat ugly peach,* I
said after I hung up.

I couldn't leave well enough alone and decided to
check my messages. The answering machine spewed out
the regular assortment of nuisance calls, with one no-
table exception.

"Mr. Nichols, this is Ms. Warden from Danny Gans
Middle School," the cheerful voice said. "I'm calling to
confirm your presentation to our eighth grade Careers
Class on Thursday afternoon. The students are looking
forward to learning all about the advertising business."

"Shit on a flat rock!" I said to Flash, who acted like he
thought that was a good idea. I'd forgotten about this
particular commitment, made months ago in a moment
of weakness, when saying "yes" seemed far easier than
concocting some lame excuse. Well, it was too late to back
out now. I'd just have to fit it into my busy
schedule. Besides, it might be fun to poison their young
minds.

15

Progress is a funny thing, as anyone learning a new skill will tell you. It's never a slow steady climb to the top, like the make-believe revenue projections at the ad agency. In real life, one day you're up, the next day you're down. You reach a certain level of success, then settle on a plateau or even backslide a bit, before taking some inexplicable leap to entirely new heights. It was a wholly mysterious process as far as I was concerned. Angela kept reminding me I had no choice but to go with it.

"You just worry about doing the right thing," she said. "All that other stuff will take care of itself."

"Yes, Obi-Won, the force is with me."

On Wednesday, the force was in another time zone. I felt awkward, like I'd never even seen a basketball, let alone shot one. My balance was shaky, my feet (all four of them) kept getting tangled up, and some rip in the cosmic fabric sent the ball ping-ponging into an endless assortment of undiscovered dimensions. I may as well have been playing in the Bermuda Triangle.

"My biorhythms are off," I said, by way of explanation.

"Those aren't the only things that are off," Angela said. "I'm sending you to the showers."

"Are you serious?"

"As a heart attack. I've seen this sort of thing before. When it all goes bad at once, it's better to just call it off. Tomorrow's another day."

"Want to get some lunch?"

"You buying?"

"Sure. I'm buying. But I get to choose."

"Go for it."

"How about deli? I'm in the mood for some Jewish soul food."

Angela gave me a puzzled look. "You're Jewish?"

"Yeah. What of it?" I asked defensively.

"Nothing. It's just ..."

Here it comes, I thought. "Just what?"

"Well, you don't look Jewish."

"Is that right? So tell me, what's a Jew supposed to look like?"

"You know, big nose, curly hair."

"What a bigot. Have you ever heard me say 'you don't look Black'?"

"That would be dumb."

"True. Still, most Jews look just like everybody else. They even have Ethiopian and Chinese Jews."

She considered it. "How come you don't have one of those Jewish names that ends in *Berg* or *Stein*?"

"My Pop told me it used to be Nicowitz. They changed it when my grandfather came through Ellis Island."

"I guess I haven't known many Jews in my life. Just some old patients at the hospital and they were obnoxious. 'Noice!' they'd yell; that's how they pronounced *nurse*. 'Noice! Bring me some ice chips. My blanket's too scratchy. Turn up the heat.' Too cold, they were always too cold. One time, this really old man calls out, 'Noice, I can't see, I can't see.' So I walk over and you know what I tell him?"

"No, what?"

"Isaac, open your eyes."

"You're joking," I managed to say between guffaws.

"May God strike me dead."

"Be honest," I said. "Were the Jews worse than your other patients?"

"Not really. Maybe a little. I don't know. Stop asking me trick questions. You tell me, how many people of color do you know?

I pretended to think for a moment. "Counting you?"

"Yes."

"That would be one."

"I rest my case."

"See, this is good for us. A little cultural exchange program."

"If you say so."

"Come on, I'm gonna teach you about fancy eating."

We left Angela's car in the rec center parking lot and headed for the Neon Deli on East Flamingo, about two miles from the Strip. On the way over, she peppered me with questions about being Jewish. It's not like I'm an authority. In fact, I only go to temple for weddings and funerals. Truth be known, I'm an epicurean Jew – strictly in it for the food. But I handled the barrage in my usual manner. Whatever I didn't know, I made up.

"What do Jews believe in, anyway?" she asked.

"God. We invented Him, you know. Before us, everybody prayed to rocks and trees. Too bad we didn't copyright the idea. You'd all be paying us a fortune in royalties. Same with the Old Testament and the Ten Commandments."

"How about Jesus?"

"A Jew. One of our boys made good."

"I always thought he was black."

"He might've been, but he was still Jewish. I'm sure he wasn't a blonde blue-eyed pretty boy like in those paintings. I mean, he lived in the desert. No SPF thirty or anything. By the way, the Last Supper was a seder."

"A what?"

"Passover dinner."

"I've heard of Passover. What is it?"

"It's a holiday celebrating when the Jews escaped from slavery in Egypt."

"Jews were slaves?"

"Yeah, everybody wanted free work out of us. See, we've got a lot in common. Didn't you ever watch 'The Ten Commandments' with Charlton Heston? He played Moses. Not Malone."

"Never heard of it."

"Get it on video. But pee first. It's about four hours long."

"But Jews don't pray to Jesus, right?"

"No. We figure, why use a middleman, when we can go right to the head honcho."

"So you don't do Christmas."

"No, we celebrate Hanukkah. It's an okay holiday, but it can't hold a candle to Christmas. When I was a kid, I was jealous, because all the goyim got these really neat presents—bikes and skateboards and things—and all I got was some chocolate coins. I think Christmas is the main reason Jews feel like outsiders."

"What's that word? *Goy* something?"

"Goyim. It means gentiles, non-Jews. You know, everybody that's not us."

"So what about Thanksgiving?"

"That's a national holiday, not a religious one. We take the whole four days off. Unless you're in the friggin' advertising business. Then you're lucky to get a Swanson Hungry Man dinner. Hey, I oughta be charging you for all this valuable info."

"Yeah, I heard Jews were fond of money."

"Some are, some aren't. I always leave a really big tip, just so people won't call me a cheap Jew bastard."

"I know what you mean. When I'm around white people, I try to sound extra articulate." She over-enunciated the word.

"So there you go."

I pulled the car into the deli lot and parked in the first available space.

"I hope you're hungry," I said. "If there's one thing

Jews know about, it's huge portions."

The Neon Deli occupies the corner position in one of Las Vegas' endless strip malls, between a souvenir shop and one of those mailbox places. When you walk in, the first thing you notice is row upon row of framed black and white photos of washed-up celebrities. "Love & Knishes, signed Marty Allen." "To Sid, Thanks for All the Kreplach, signed Shecky Greene." "Danke Schoen, signed Wayne Newton." (Not a Jew, as Adam Sandler would say. Nobody's sure what he is.) Other than that, the place is a dump. Wobbly tables, ripped booths, garage-sale-quality silverware. Our waitress, Sharon from Brooklyn, has been there since the day it opened, some twenty years ago. It's impossible to catch her eye. She wouldn't shake a leg if a dog was hanging off it. But the food is so damned good, it just doesn't matter. And I wasn't kidding about the portions.

Angela seemed overwhelmed by the menu, which is roughly the size of the Vegas white pages.

"I never heard of a lot of this stuff. What's a lox?"

"Smoked salmon. Very salty. It's an acquired taste."

"Look at this, beef tongue. You eat that? It sounds disgusting."

"I agree. My dad used to order it every now and then, and it looks even worse than it sounds. One thing I can tell you, cows have huge taste buds."

She made a face.

"And you don't even want to know about gefilte fish."

"Filthy fish?"

"That's pretty much it."

"Now here's something I'm familiar with. Corned beef. I get that at the supermarket."

"Not like this corned beef, I'll bet."

"It's pretty good. Leon's, that's what it's called."

I stuck out my tongue. "That crap is depressed and deformed. The corned beef they serve here is the Real McCoy."

"OK, I'll get a corned-beef sandwich."

"Can I make a suggestion?"

"You always do."

"Order half a sandwich and a cup of matzo ball soup."

"What ball soup?"

"Matzo ball. It's homemade chicken soup with a big fluffy dumpling. Delicious. They call it Jewish penicillin, because all our mothers made it when we were sick."

"You talked me into it. Are you sure a half sandwich is enough?"

"I guarantee you've never seen a half sandwich like this one. If you finish it and want another, be my guest. You're a better person than I am."

"Goes without saying."

At last, Sharon from Brooklyn drifted over. Everything's fake on Sharon, from her hair color to her boobs.

"You folks ready to order?" she asked in her nasally New York accent.

"Yes." As an aside, I whispered to Angela, "Don't send her away, or you'll never see her again."

"What'll you have, hon?"

"I'd like half a corned beef sandwich and a cup of that soup with the dumpling."

Sharon frowned.

"She means matzo ball," I said helpfully. "You'll have to excuse my cousin. She's from Sweden."

Sharon appeared skeptical. "Really. What part of Sweden?"

"South Central," Angela said.

"Oh." Without missing a beat, Sharon asked, "Bread?"

"Huh?" Angela asked, bewildered.

"Bread. For your sandwich. What kind?"

"The regular kind," Angela said. "You know, white bread."

"Hold on just a second," I interrupted. "Nobody eats corned beef on white." I turned to Sharon. "Is the rye fresh?"

"Of course."

"She'll have that. Mustard, no mayo. I'll have the same. And bring us a side of new dills."

"You got it."

After Sharon left, Angela asked, "What's wrong with white bread? I've been eating it all my life."

"Have you heard the expression, 'When in Rome'?"

"Uh-huh."

"Just trust me."

"The last time somebody said that, my savings account got cleaned out."

Soon enough, Sharon brought our food. I watched Angela's eyes grow large as she examined the mile-high sandwich.

"Pick it up," I said. "It won't bite."

"That's a half?" she asked incredulously. "I don't think I can open my mouth that wide."

"Just relax your jaw muscles. You'll get the hang of it."

All conversation came to an abrupt halt as we attacked our meal. After a couple of false starts, Angela maneuvered her way around the sandwich like a pro. Before long, we were both making satisfied smacking and slurping sounds. Finally, when the last crumb of bread and final drop of soup were gone, she pushed her plate away and said, "Now that's some mighty fine eatin'."

"I don't want to say I told you so … "

"In fact," she continued, "that's the second best meal I've had in Las Vegas."

I took the bait. "What's the first?"

"Fat Daddy's Chicken & Ribs."

"Maybe I'll try it some time."

"Next week," she said. "Lunch is on me."

16

Whether it was the day off or the corned-beef sandwich, Thursday proved to be the exact opposite of Wednesday. I started out at a sixty-percent clip from three-point land and never looked back. Whatever mojo I had working lasted all morning. I wished I could somehow transport myself to the actual million-dollar contest in the blink of an eye, like on 'I Dream of Jeannie.' It reminded me of the days when I used to practice blackjack strategy at home with Pam or a friend. Unfortunately, my hot streaks never found their way into a casino. Casinos are where luck goes to die.

"I look like a genius out here," I told Angela. She was not impressed.

As a rule, Angela and I are the only ones in the rec center until after lunch, when the elementary-school kids take over. Today, I was in such a groove that we stayed later than usual, drawing a crowd of young onlookers. After I knocked down eight straight shots, a wide-eyed boy of ten or so came over and said, "Gee, Mister, you're really good. Did you ever play in the NBA?"

Other than my wedding and the birth of my daughter, that might've been the highlight of my life. Beaming at the lad, I said, "As a matter of fact, I did. Have you ever heard of the Big O?"

"The tire store?"

"The ball player."

"Nope."

"Well, that's me. Go home and tell your parents you met Oscar Robertson."

"Cool!"

As he ran off to join his friends, Angela could only shake her head and mutter, "You're outta control."

"Oh, let me have a little fun."

She turned serious. "You listen to me. What you're doin' here, it ain't nothin'. When it's crunch time and your hands are sweatin' and your heart's poundin' right out of your chest and you step up to the line and make your shot, then you got braggin' rights. Not before."

"Okay, okay. Ease up. What's got into you?"

"Yesterday you stunk, today you're Mr. Basketball. Which is it? Neither. You better respect the game or it'll turn on you."

"All right already. I'll be good, I promise."

"That's more like it."

"I guess this is a lousy time to tell you, but I've gotta run. I'm speaking about advertising to a class of eighth-graders."

"Just don't tell them you're Oscar Robertson."

I made a few mental notes about my ex-profession on the way to Danny Gans Middle School, on the east side of town between Las Vegas and Henderson. Although I had never been to this particular campus, it brought back memories, because it looked exactly like Amy's alma mater. As far as I can tell, all Clark County middle schools are built on the identical floor plan: a circular hub-and-spokes design, giving it the appearance of a spaceship from one of those 1950s B movies. Thinking back to Amy's parent-teacher conferences, I remembered the halls being one-way, presumably to expedite the flow of traffic. If your next class was to the immediate left of the one you just completed, you had to walk around the entire circle to get there. A stupid rule, but good practice for the outside world.

I checked in at the office with a girl of about thirteen, who directed me to Ms. Warden's class. Just for fun, I made a left turn, heading upstream against the rush of students, drawing some dirty looks in the process. I half expected one of the campus cops to shout "Halt" and draw his gun, dropping me where I stood. Pam would read about me in tomorrow's paper. "I had no choice," the guard would be quoted as saying. "He was going the wrong way." The school district would likely give him a commendation and promotion, while my bullet-riddled body lay on a cold slab at the morgue.

Fortunately, I made it to class in once piece, taking a deep breath before pulling on the handle. I don't care how long you've been out of school. Walking into class is still a nerve-wracking experience.

Ms. Warden was a petite brunette easily fifteen years my junior. I'm always surprised by how much younger the teachers appear these days. They look more like teaching assistants. Or students.

I smiled and introduced myself. "I'm Alan Nichols, here to talk about advertising."

"Denise Warden," she said, offering her hand. "Thank you so much for coming. You'll be our second speaker, just after Captain Michael Edwards of the Air Force Thunderbirds. I hope you don't mind. We were lucky to get him at the last minute."

Mind? Why should I mind? This was only a jet pilot from the world famous elite precision aerobatic mother-fucking Thunderbirds. Out of the corner of my eye, I could see the macho image of the swashbuckling captain, cutting quite a figure in his crisp dress uniform. Already, the boys and girls were watching him expectantly, albeit for different reasons. But all I could think to say was, "Maybe it would be better if I came back another time. We could reschedule."

"Don't be silly," Ms. Warden said. "The students are very interested in advertising. Just take a seat and relax, and we'll be ready for you shortly."

I slunk away to the back of the class and wedged myself in between a boy with severe acne and a big-boned girl. While the jet jockey droned on about stunt flying at Mach 2, I took the time to study the students. Although the clothes and hairstyles and accessories were different, the basic types remained the same. Even in eighth grade, you could identify the budding jocks, cheerleaders, and homecoming royalty, as well as the nerds, geeks, and other assorted misfits. For some, the public school system would be the peak experience of their lives, while most would emerge scarred and itching for revenge, either by making a ton of money or by shooting a helpless convenience-store clerk. You never can tell. I'm sure Bill Gates wasn't voted "Most Likely to Succeed." Neither was Jeffrey Dahmer. In any event, the students were lucky to be unaware of the surprises the world had in store for them. Not long after my Pop died, I remember leafing through his high-school yearbook. It was just before graduation, and the autographs said things like "Go get 'em!" and "Let's make some real dough." That was in June 1941, six months before Pearl Harbor. Less than a year later, he was on the USS Hornet heading for the battle of Midway.

I was startled out of my mental meanderings by the sound of applause. Captain Michael Edwards was done. You always had to watch out for the guys with the short Anglo-Saxon names. Mike, Rick, Chuck. Those were real men. Names like Barry, Neil, Mitchell, you could kick their ass. Or Alan. That's why I preferred "Nick," although I wasn't fooling anybody.

After a short break, during which I snuck out for a pint of orange juice and a chocolate cookie, Ms. Warden handled my introduction.

"People, settle down. Eyes front. Feet on the floor.

Our next guest comes to us from the world of advertising. Please give your full attention to Mr. Alan Nichols."

I walked to the front of the classroom amidst total silence. Looking out at the faces, I could see they shared a common bond. Boredom.

"Thank you for that warm welcome." Nothing. Obviously, sarcasm was lost on them. "How many of you watch TV?" A few hands shot right up, slowly followed by the rest of the class.

"Good. The networks will be pleased. Now, do any of you have a favorite commercial? Don't all speak up at once." After a painful pause, one student cautiously raised his hand.

"I like the beer commercial with the twins." A few assorted snickers of recognition, along with a "Me too," from somebody.

"Excellent. Anybody else?"

A girl said, "The Hallmark commercials during the holidays. They make me cry."

"That's what they're supposed to do, work on your emotions. Fear, guilt, love, greed. Let me ask you this. What commercials do you totally hate?" This elicited a more immediate response.

"That English car salesman."

"The furniture guy who yells all the time."

"The bald lawyer."

The list went on and on. Finally, I said, "Great. Can anybody tell me where these commercials come from?"

"Hell!" a voice shouted from the back of the room. Riotous laughter.

Ms. Warden shot up like a jack-in-the-box. "Josh, I'll see you after class." Josh slithered down in his seat.

"Actually, he's not that far off," I said. "They come from places called advertising agencies. Ad agencies are where specially trained employees meet with businesses called clients, and develop the campaigns you see on TV, in magazines and newspapers, on billboards, and everywhere else. Did you know that, by the time you're twenty-one, you'll be exposed to a million different advertising messages?" A murmur swept the room. "That's right. They're training you how to be good little consumers. Without advertising, how would you know which products to buy?"

"Ads don't work on me," one boy interrupted. "I think for myself." This was good. I was starting to get them involved.

"Of course you do. What's your favorite soft drink?" I asked him.

"Sprite."

"Why is that?"

"Because I obey my thirst," he said, parroting the company slogan. The rest of the class laughed. Even Ms. Warden cracked a tiny grin.

"Exactly," I told him. "We're all brainwashed by ads. Most of us aren't aware of it, that's all. Do you know one of the first phrases a toddler says, after 'mommy' and 'daddy'?"

"What?"

"Buy me that."

I went on to talk briefly about ad strategy and agency structure and the importance of a good education, especially language skills, which made them all groan. Finally, it was time for a few questions. After the usual query about salaries, one boy with close-cropped hair and a letterman's jacket asked, "Aren't you the guy who won the million-dollar basketball shot?"

"Yes. How'd you recognize me?"

"I saw you on the news. Sweet." He said it like "sa-weet …"

"Do you play?" I asked him.

"Sure do," he said proudly, pointing to his jacket. "Varsity."

"Any words of wisdom?"

"Don't miss."

The ringing of the bell drowned out any additional advice.

"That wasn't so bad," I thought, as I headed back to the car. On the way, I passed by the playground, now completely deserted. The sun played hide-and-seek behind some rain clouds, keeping the temperature slightly lower than normal. "What the hell," I said out loud, and grabbed my basketball from the back seat. After taking off my suit coat and tie and tossing them over a bench, I stationed myself at the top of the key. This basket had a chain instead of a net, and it clanked as the ball sailed through. I glanced around furtively, thinking the noise might have attracted attention. But there was nobody to hear it, except a lone pigeon munching on the remnants of an Oreo cookie. "Just one more shot," I said dozens of times. Before I knew it, I was inventing scenarios to keep myself involved, the kind of mind games I hadn't played since I was a kid.

"If Alan Nichols sinks this next one," I said to myself, "he'll not only win the million dollars, he'll live forever." Not even close. "Okay, two out of three." Sometimes I ruled the world, but mostly the devil stole my soul. Luckily, there was always another shot, another chance to get it right. I kept it up for I don't know how long, lost in the moment, oblivious to the after-school onslaught, until the playground monitor stopped by and asked me to please go home.

17

"So, are you going to do it?" Pam asked me.

"Do what?"

"Bungee jump. Tomorrow's Saturday. You promised Jason."

"I did nothing of the sort. I said I'd check it out."

"And then what?"

"Then I'll say no."

"Maybe I should come along. Just in case."

"Suit yourself. After I tell him to forget it, we can have a nice breakfast."

Just then, Amy came flying downstairs, her long mane of blonde hair trailing behind her like so many streamers. She looked more like Pam every day. "Hi Mom, hi Dad. Bye Mom, bye Dad. Late for work."

"Drive safely!" I shouted in the direction of the slamming door. "Don't slam."

I finished my last sip of coffee. "I'd better be going, too. See you around." I gave Pam a dramatic movie-style kiss.

"Keep that up and you'll never get out of here." If it hadn't been so close to crunch time, I would've called in sick.

When I got to the gym, Angela said, "This week sure went by fast."

"It sure did."

"Tomorrow's Saturday."

"Yep."

"The big day."

"Knock if off. I'm not jumping, okay?"

"I didn't say you were."

"All right, then."

"All right. Get to work."

After missing my first three attempts, I slammed the ball on the floor and stomped over to Angela. "What's the big deal?" I asked. "I still don't see what bungee jumping has to do with basketball."

"I told you at dinner. It's not necessarily bungee jumping. It could be anything. Whatever you're most afraid of."

"I'm a schmuck. I should've said I'm scared of sitting on the beach in Hawaii, sipping piña coladas."

"Too late now."

"Doesn't matter. I'm not doing it."

"I never said you were. But I'm coming anyway."

"You'll be disappointed."

"I'll take that chance."

When I got home, I was again disappointed by the mail. I lurched for the phone and called Ginger, pacing back and forth across the kitchen floor, somehow managing to avoid Flash's tail. I was going to give that bitch a piece of my mind. Except that I got voicemail.

"It's Nick," I said with controlled fury. "Call me. I don't care how late." I slammed down the receiver. It's never a good idea to unload on voicemail, no matter how mad you are. It could come back to haunt you—in a court of law.

Now what? Should I call Dunbar? I was hoping to avoid him for the rest of my life. But the voice in my head, the one I never listen to, was screaming that this was more than an honest mistake. I listened to it just long enough to make the call. The receptionist was new. She informed me that Joe Dunbar "is in a meeting and is not to be disturbed." How about Jason McBride? Gone for the day. Did I want voicemail?

I called Jason's cell phone instead. He answered on the first ring.

"Thank God you're there."

"That's usually what the girls say. What's up, Nick?"

"I never got my final check. Is there any more of that suspicious shit going on?"

"Nope. Unless you count endless closed-door meetings. To be honest with you, we're all a little spooked."

"Well, do me a favor. See what you can find out. I think Ginger knows something."

"Ginger always knows something."

"Maybe you could bang it out of her."

Jason laughed, but I could tell it was forced. "Talk about taking one for the team."

"Let's hope it doesn't come to that."

"See you tomorrow," Jason said.

Damn, I was hoping he forgot.

Tomorrow arrived at warp speed. Why does time move so quickly when you don't want it to? Meanwhile, that last minute on the school clock always lasted an eternity. Too bad Einstein's dead. He could have explained it to me.

"Good morning!" Jason sang cheerfully when I opened the door a crack.

"Go away."

"Come in," Pam told him over my shoulder.

He asked, "Ready for a life-changing experience?"

"I got your life-changing experience right here."

"You'll thank me when it's over."

"It's *already* over."

"Come on," he urged. "I'm driving."

Pam yelled for Amy, "Are you joining us?"

"Wouldn't miss it."

"We'll follow you boys," Pam said. "I'm sure you have lots to talk about."

No sooner had I put a little distance between the girls and myself, I whispered to Jason, "Don't say a word to Pam about my last paycheck. I don't want her to worry."

Jason gave me the thumbs-up sign. As we headed for our vehicles, Angela pulled up in her big blue boat. The brakes made a metal-on-metal screech as she angled toward the curb.

"Morning, y'all," she said. "I was in the neighborhood and thought I'd drop by."

"Like hell you were," I said.

"We were just going for a little drive," Pam said. "Want to join us?"

"You know it, girl."

When you live in Las Vegas, you try to avoid the Fabulous Strip at all costs. I'm sure people from Orlando don't go to Disney World, either. It's either a parking lot or a demolition derby. On the Strip, out-of-town drivers aim right for your car. "Look at all the lights, Martha," the husband says, as he's running you off the road. On this ill-fated Saturday morning, I was praying for a traffic jam of epic proportions. Of course, we sailed right through.

The Bungee World platform rises nineteen stories above the Strip, directly in front of the Circus Circus Hotel-Casino. When I first came to town, I thought Circus Circus was the tackiest, and therefore funniest, of all the major resort properties. "Would you like a room with or without an elephant?" I pictured the reservation girl asking. Now, the place struck me as an idea whose time has come and gone. Compared to a replica of New York City, or a thirty-story glass pyramid, or the nation's tallest freestanding tower, a clown and some trapeze artists aren't exactly cutting edge.

Like most everything else in Vegas, the Bungee World office has a theme. The walls are made of paper mache rocks. A fake waterfall, not much bigger than a backyard pool accessory, adorns one corner of the room. The front desk is decorated like a thatched hut, the employees decked out in jungle khakis and pith helmets. All designed to enhance that overall sense of adventure, as if flinging yourself off a 190-foot platform isn't adventure enough.

Jason marched up to the counter with me trailing badly behind and announced our arrival. "McBride, party of two," he said, as if this were some fancy restaurant, not the instrument of our impending destruction. In keeping with the jungle theme, the desk girl was of Amazonian proportions, easily over six feet tall. She smiled and said, "You don't need to be so formal, Jason. It's not like you're a stranger around here. We're all ready for you."

"I'm not jumping," I protested, my voice a croak.

The girl kept smiling. "Just watch the video. Then you can decide."

"It's only a video," Jason added.

"Yeah, Dad," Amy chimed in. "We all want to see it."

Amazon Girl led us to an alcove where a big-screen TV was set up. She popped in a disk, hit the play button, and the screen flickered to life. We were treated to a montage of scenes from exotic locales the world over. Bungee jumpers jumping from bridges. Bungee jumpers jumping from hot air balloons. Bungee jumpers jumping from cliffs. The breezy background music added to the impression of safe lighthearted fun.

"I guess they edit out the crash landings," I commented.

"We've never had an accident at Bungee World," Amazon Girl insisted. She obviously took her work seriously.

The next section was hosted by a rugged deeply tanned bloke with an Australian accent who went over the safety precautions in great detail. "At Bungee World, we use two harnesses, one around your ankles, and another around your waist, for extra protection." It reminded me of an ad I once worked on. For condoms.

"That's a relief," I said.

"Ssshhh," Angela said. "We're trying to watch."

The last part featured testimonials by happy jumpers who used the word "awesome" a lot. Too quickly, the demo ended and I noticed everyone eyeing me curiously.

"I just realized, I forgot my checkbook."

"All taken care of," Jason assured me.

Amazon Girl instructed, "You just have to sign the release form."

The release form is the second scariest part of bungee jumping. It's an imposing multi-page document containing the usual stuff about bad backs, weak necks, and faint hearts.

"I have all those," I claimed.

"No, he doesn't, he's healthy as a horse," Pam said.

"Whose side are you on?" I wanted to know.

"No sides. You're on your own."

The next clause spelled out the weight restrictions. Nobody under 100 pounds or over 250 pounds. For the first time in my life, I wished I was fat. But it was the item about eyes that grabbed me. Something about them popping out.

"What's this all about?" I demanded.

"Oh, that," Amazon Girl pooh-poohed. "That almost never happens. It's not statistically relevant."

"Then why put it in?"

"It's from the legal department."

"Let *them* jump. I'm not signing it."

Jason said, "You have to, or they won't let you ride up the elevator. Don't you want to see what it looks like from up there?"

"Not especially."

"If you go up in the elevator and you decide you don't want to go through with it, I won't say a word. Okay?"

"Sounds reasonable."

"It's too late to get my money back, anyway."

"Guilt will get you nowhere."

"I know."

Before we could get into the elevator, I was ushered over to a large scale.

"It's so we know how long of a cord to use," Amazon Girl explained. "A hundred sixty-five pounds," she said.

"Very good."

"Just tell me one thing," I said. "Am I the oldest person you've seen around here?"

She smiled. "No way. Last month, we had a grandmother celebrating her eightieth birthday."

"Where'd you stash the body?"

I said my good byes to wife, daughter, and coach.

"I love you," from Pam.

"Good luck, Dad," from Amy.

"Keep it real," from Angela.

Not *too* real, from myself.

Soon after, Jason and I found ourselves in one of those old-fashioned open-air elevators. Our guide was a burley kid of nineteen or twenty. The name badge identified him as "Cliff." How appropriate, I thought. The elevator creaked along slowly, but it was still too fast for me. When the latticework door slid open, I had my first epiphany. Things seem even higher when you're looking down.

Cliff asked, "Who wants to go first?"

"He does," Jason and I both said, pointing at each other.

"Now wait just a goddamn minute," I said angrily. "You promised."

"I know. But if you don't go now, you'll never go."

"That's the general idea."

"This is your moment of truth."

I swallowed hard. Maybe he was right. Maybe the time had come to do something completely out of character. I mean, how tough could it be, if grandmothers were doing it? Besides, if it would help me make my shot ...

Finally, I said, "All right. But if anything happens to me, you're taking care of my family for the rest of your miserable life."

Jason grinned. "I'm all over it."

Before I knew it, I was wearing a double protective harness, my legs bound tighter than any prisoner's.

"I'm going to count backwards from three," Cliff said in a voice that suddenly seemed far away. "When I reach zero, hold your arms out in front of you and fall forward. Don't jump, but don't hesitate either, or you'll probably chicken out. And remember, we won't push you. You have to do this on your own. Any questions?"

"What if I throw up?"

"It's impossible to throw up when you're upside down."

Another interesting tidbit if I'm ever on "Jeopardy."

With my ankles shackled together, I inched forward using little baby steps, until my shoes were halfway over the platform. It was a bright sunny morning and the vast sprawl of Las Vegas stretched out before me. In both directions, construction cranes loomed above the landscape like giant metal dinosaurs. Later, when I watched the video (Jason had popped for the deluxe package), I saw the face of pure terror. My face. No condemned man ever looked more frightened.

Glancing down, I could make out the tiny figures of Pam, Amy, and Angela, standing next to a postage stamp-sized swimming pool. I waved, realizing that my hands were colder than they'd ever been. They waved back, or maybe they were just praying. From up here, it was hard to tell.

Now I could hear the countdown. "Three." My brain, the rational part, began a last-ditch effort to talk me out of it. "You're not really going through with this, are you?" it demanded. "Two." "You're gonna get us both killed." "One." "No, we have to live, so we can kill Jason." Zero. "This isn't funny. Stop it. NOW!" I took a deep breath, told my brain to get lost, and lunged forward.

The first part of the jump was in slow motion, like Wile E. Coyote right after he runs off the cliff, before he realizes he's fucked. Frame by frozen frame it went, until my feet had completely separated from the platform. Then, with a sudden "whoosh," gravity grabbed me with a vengeance, literally yanking me toward the ground. I was plummeting faster than any falling nightmare, a mad rush of colors and shapes whizzing past my eyes, my poor brain screaming "NO NO NO!" in horror and disbelief. At last, the cord fully engaged about ten feet above the swimming pool, and I came to an almost complete stop before getting boinged upward at an impossible angle, my arms flailing away crazily like a scarecrow in a windstorm. As I zoomed back toward the platform, I said a quick "thank you" to whatever deity might be on call and made a mental note never to commit suicide by jumping. At the top of my first rebound, feeling weightless for a fraction of a second, I actually had the presence of mind to admire the scenery before gravity again took over and sent me spinning wildly in another direction.

"He's having a great jump," I heard somebody say. Lucky me.

After three more boings, each less jarring than the one before, I came to a stop, hanging upside down like a tree bat, maybe twenty feet off the ground. Reaching up with a long metal pole, a husky employee carefully guided me to the safety of a mat next to the swimming pool. As I lay there, the bile rising in my throat, I conducted a mental inventory of body parts (especially my eyes), and waited for the blood to return to my extremities. All at once, I was surrounded by three familiar figures.

"Are you okay?" Pam asked. She looked as shaken as I felt.

"I guess."

"Let's go home."

"Good idea."

"Promise me you won't do that again."

That's one promise I'd have no trouble keeping.

18

That night, just before I fell asleep, the little man in my head, the one who never missed a shot, fell off a building. Each time I closed my eyes, the mental images became more and more jumbled, morphing into a weird mishmash of nightmarish scenes. Sometimes, he plunged down an elevator shaft just after shooting the ball. Other times, he tumbled headfirst into one of those deserted mines, the basketball ricocheting off the walls into the darkness. Always, I snapped out of my semi-dream state with a jolt, my heart doing some insane tap dance in my chest.

Still, I had to admit, I didn't regret the jump. I found that the experience energized me, recharged my batteries at a very deep level. Perhaps Angela was right after all. I looked fear straight in the eye and didn't blink. Sure, I *whined* a little, but that's just my style. And that was beside the point. I took my college diploma down from our den wall and proudly hung my "Bungee Certificate of Valor" in its place. Just don't ask me to jump again, I thought, as I tossed the punch card in the trash. Sure, I was developing that intangible thing called "attitude," but no need to get crazy about it.

As it turned out, I'd need all the attitude I could get. That's because, first thing Monday morning, the shit hit the fan. I'd just settled in at the kitchen table with a cup of coffee and the dreaded *Post*. After breezing through the Sports section, I turned my attention to Business, where the headline blared "Agency Seeks Bankruptcy Protection." At first, it didn't register. Agency? What agency? Car-rental agency? Employment agency? It could be anything. But the type was so large, I decided it must be worth a look. The first paragraph read, "In a stunning move that took industry insiders by surprise, Dunbar and Associates, Las Vegas' largest advertising agency, filed a motion on Friday seeking Chapter 11 bankruptcy protection. The firm, with annual revenues of more than $162 million, represents Paragon Gaming Group, Valley Automotive Center, and the Galaxy Mall, among others. Undisclosed sources speculate that the agency had lost a number of key accounts in recent weeks. Phone calls to CEO Joseph Dunbar, 65, were not immediately returned."

There was plenty more, but I couldn't deal with it. My mind was spinning in too many different directions at once. From what I knew about Chapter 11, I wouldn't be getting my final check anytime soon. A hardship, certainly, but by no means a disaster. I still had the million dollar-shot to look forward to. Even if I missed, the $50,000 consolation prize (minus Jason's and Angela's shares) would get us over the rough spots. And I could always file for unemployment. Dunbar might dispute it, but I had a feeling he had more important things on his mind.

The more immediate concern was what to tell Pam, if anything. I'm not a big believer in keeping secrets from my wife. On the other hand, I didn't want her to worry unnecessarily. (Or to somehow find a way to make this my fault.) It was a moot point. As soon as I heard her footsteps on the stairs, some primal male instinct took over. The one that screams, "hide the evidence!" With maybe three seconds to spare, I deep-sixed the Business section at the bottom of the trashcan, under some particularly nasty garbage. Then, just as she made her appearance, I tipped the can over, sending coffee grounds and chicken bones skidding across the floor. From his spot in the corner, Flash gave them a token glance before deciding it wasn't worth getting up.

Pam eyed me with bemusement. "A little jumpy, aren't we?"

"Too much coffee," I said. She made a move to help pick up the mess but I cut her off. "I've got it!"

She took a step back. "Okay, okay. I don't know what's gotten into you this morning."

"It's just that you look so nice, I don't want you to get all dirty."

She regarded me suspiciously. "That's very considerate. Well, I'm off to Grant-a-Wish. By the way, I might have a surprise for you tonight."

"I hate surprises."

"You'll like this one." She gave me a peck on the lips and turned to leave. As the door closed behind her, the phone rang and I knocked over the trash again.

"I've got big news," said Jason McBride.

"Let me guess," I said, peeking out the window to make sure Pam wasn't coming back. "Dunbar's bankrupt."

Silence. Then, "How'd you know?"

"Lucky guess. Also, it's plastered all over the Business section." I let out a small sigh of relief as Pam got into her car and drove off.

"Damn. I banged Ginger for nothing."

"You're kidding, right?" The mental picture of Ginger naked made me cringe.

"Yeah, I'm kidding. But I had to be really nice to her. It took ten years off my life."

"Well, I appreciate it."

"So, what do you think'll happen now? Will I still have a job?"

"I'm no expert," I answered carefully. "But I'm pretty sure they'll try to keep the doors open. Chapter eleven gives them a chance to get back on their feet. I just don't know what the time frame will be."

"I can't afford to miss too many paydays."

"A young single guy like you?"

"That's the problem. It costs money being a young single guy like me." He paused. "Of course, if you make your shot, I've got nothing to worry about."

"Right." Instantly, I could feel my shoulder muscles tighten up.

"Well, don't let me keep you from the gym," he said with forced good cheer. "Eye of the tiger."

We hung up. Jason was a good kid and I wanted to help him out, but I really didn't need this added stress. He was right about one thing, though. I couldn't wait to get back to the rec center and forget about everything. Everything, that is, except putting the ball through the hole.

19

The rec center was not the trouble-free haven I'd been hoping for. Far from it. For one thing, Angela was nowhere to be seen. That wasn't like her. I filed away my concern in the same place I stash my worries about colorectal cancer and decided to take some warm up shots. In my current frame of mind, I was lucky to hit the backboard, let alone the basket. After ten shots, I was ohfer. I was about to miss number eleven when a familiar voice disrupted my lack of flow. "You don't remember one thing I taught you."

I spun around to find Angela in street clothes, her hair a disheveled mess, her eyes red-rimmed and hollow.

"You look like I feel," I said, trying to lighten the mood. "Tough night?"

"The toughest," she said in a frayed monotone. "I went out for a few drinks with my girlfriend Fontina. When I got back, the front door was open and all my stuff was gone. Color TV, stereo, laptop, everything. Even Spanky, my cat." Her lower lip trembled, but there was no other outward sign of emotion. "It's Clyde, I know it. If I run into that sucker, I'm gonna go Lorena Bobbitt on his ass. Among other places."

"I'm sorry," I said, and I meant it. But that didn't stop me from worrying about how this was going to affect *me*. Deep down, I'm not always the great guy I think I am. "What's Metro say?"

She laughed bitterly. "That's a joke. The cop said he hopes I got insurance."

"Do you?"

"What do you think? This is a big setback. I'll be lucky if I can pay the rent."

I took a breath and asked the question I was dreading. "What'll you do now?"

"Go on home, I guess."

I knew the answer even before I said, "To an empty apartment?"

"Detroit."

I grimaced.

Her expression softened for the first time since entering the gym. "I'm sorry, Nick. I know we had a deal, but I gotta get outta here. The writing's all over the wall."

My heart sank and my words spilled out too fast. "Please, Angela, we'll figure something out. I can't do this without you."

"Stop talkin' crazy, of course you can. It's not like I'm the only coach in town."

"You're the only coach for me."

We just stood there for a few seconds, staring at each other. Finally, she said, "Nick, it's over. Thanks for everything."

With surprising quickness, I stepped between her and the door. "Wait! What if we find you another apartment? Furnished. In a really nice part of town, like Anthem or Summerlin. Clyde'll never look for you there."

Angela shook her head slowly. "You weren't listening. No way I can afford it."

I swallowed hard and took the plunge. "I'll pay. How about an advance on your final two weeks? And whatever else you need."

I could see the wheels spinning in her head and I thought I had a puncher's chance. Finally, she said, "I can't let you do that." She pivoted past me with catlike agility.

"Consider it a loan, then!" I shouted after her.

"I'll think about it!" she called back before disappearing through the door.

"Besides," I said quietly. "You still owe me lunch."

20

I know it like I know my own name, a lesson I learned early in my advertising career. Handle the little problems before they become big ones. Don't sweep them under the rug, where they'll have a nice quiet place to fester and ripen and grow. Because, sure as I'm a balding, middle-aged, out-of-work Jew, they'll find a way to bite you in the ass. That's what I was thinking when I came home and plopped myself down on the couch. The *new* couch. Soft and supple, chocolate brown, big as Angela's Oldsmobile. And just about the most comfortable piece of furniture this side of Baby Bear's bed. I could spend the rest of my life on that couch.

Two problems. First, we couldn't afford it. This morning, if I'd stepped up to the plate and told Pam about the bankruptcy, the couch wouldn't be an issue. It wouldn't even be here; one phone call and it would have never left the showroom floor. No harm, no foul, as we say in the basketball biz. Too late now. Inevitably, feelings were going to be hurt. One of us would end the night in tears and one of us would feel like a shitheel. Maybe I'd wind up sleeping on the couch. As I tenderly stroked the armrest, it occurred to me that this wasn't such a bad idea. You had to look for the silver lining, right?

Second, new purchases led to more new purchases. It reminded me of the legendary Nichols family bathroom-vanity story, a cautionary tale if there ever was one. Years ago, our neighbor Charlie Galloway found himself in the middle of a major home remodeling project. At the last minute, his wife decided she hated their new bathroom vanity. It looked perfectly fine to me. I took it off Charlie's hands for a hundred bucks. After Pam's brother Glen installed it for us, we realized the vanity didn't match the bathroom floor. So out went the old tiles, replaced by better, more expensive ones. Well, you couldn't have new flooring and old paint, so the bathroom walls got a new coat. Except now the bedroom walls looked like shit. Which led to more painting, new carpeting, expensive furniture, and so on. Ultimately, it spread like cancer, metastasizing through the hallway, into the other bedroom, down the stairs, taking over the kitchen and living room and den and spilling out the front door, where it finally fizzled out after two layers of exterior latex enamel. When we tallied the final costs, the bathroom vanity had set us back a good twenty-five grand. I could see it happening again. From my vantage point on the new comfy couch, the rest of the living room was looking shabby by comparison.

For the second time that day, Pam scared the crap out of me. "Surprised?" she asked.

"You can say that again," I said, after my heart resumed its normal rhythm. "I didn't hear you come in."

"Don't you just love it? It's Micro-Fiber, the hottest new thing," she beamed. I hadn't seen her this excited since ... well, maybe ever.

I eased myself up from the couch and walked over to Pam, wrapping her in my arms. "I do," I said. "I love it."

"But?" Pam questioned, looking deeply into my eyes. "I can always tell when there's a 'but.'"

I saw my opening. "You're right. I mean, we really can't afford it. Something like this has to cost, what? Four, five thousand?"

"Thirty-six hundred. On clearance. Ninety days same as cash."

"A fantastic deal. Still ..." Come on, you coward. Tell

her about the final check! "Don't forget, I'm out of work and ..." My words trailed off into nothingness.

Pam pushed herself away. "Nick, I'm reading this book called *Prosperity Consciousness*. The author says if we spend money like we have it, we'll get even more. Some kind of universal law of attraction. I can't say I totally understand it, but it's worth a try, don't you think?"

It was some great sales job. Pam was all bright-eyed and animated. Talk about a universal law of attraction. How could I say no?

"Sure," I said. "Let's see what happens." I had a pretty good idea what was going to happen, and it involved divorce and debtor's prison. "But do me one favor. Hold off on the matching chair and ottoman."

Pam wrapped herself around me and gave me a deep passionate kiss. Never was a man less deserving. "Let's try that couch on for size," she suggested, leading me by the hand. When I gave her a dubious look, she read my mind. "I had it Scotchgarded. No extra charge."

21

To recap: In only two weeks, I had managed to lose my job, my final paycheck, and my coach. And I was in the process of losing my wife, although she didn't know it yet. Not bad for a guy with no skills. As far as I was concerned, Bigg Fizz could take that bottle cap and shove it up their super-carbonated asses.

The trouble with bad news is, you don't know if you've bottomed out until it's too late. On Tuesday morning, I parked myself on our new stain-free couch and pretended to read the funnies, all the while trying to figure out my next move. Should I take another run at Angela? Look for a new coach? Practice on my own and hope for the best? And what would I tell Pam? Maybe I should keep this a secret, too. I was getting pretty good at it, if you didn't count the new crop of ulcers chewing through my stomach like organic Pac-Men.

My brain kept clinging to one life preserver of a thought. "I'm due for a break. I'm due for a break." A perfectly serviceable mantra for us nonbelievers. As if on cue, the phone rang. Reluctantly, I left the sanctuary of the couch.

"Mornin', homeboy." Angela! Was it my imagination or did she sound almost buoyant?

A lone endorphin dripped into my bloodstream. "Hey, Coach," I said, trying not to get my hopes up.

"Guess who's in jail?"

"If it's you, I'm hanging up."

"Guess again."

Another endorphin joined its predecessor. "Clyde?"

"You got that right!"

In the mirror, I caught a glimpse of somebody who looked like me. Except he was sporting a big stupid grin. "How'd you find out?"

"He called me himself. With his one phone call."

"Don't tell me," I said, the picture coming into focus.

"Yep. Asked if I'd bail his ass out."

When we were finally done laughing, I said, "There's a word for that in Yiddish. It's called *chutzpah.*"

"Hoot-spa?"

"Like the boy who kills his parents and asks the judge for mercy because he's an orphan."

"That's my Clyde, all right. Full of that hoot-spa. And other stuff."

"I wonder how they caught him."

"I understand he had himself a little too much to drink and went out and rear-ended a car. A *cop* car."

"Lucky break. For you, not Clyde."

"It gets better. He still had my stuff in the van."

"That's great!" I couldn't stop smiling. My face was starting to hurt.

"Wasn't even his van. I imagine he won't be bothering me again for some time. So it looks like I'm back in the coaching business."

"You won't regret it," I assured her.

"I regret it already. Get your skinny white ass over to the gym in a half-hour. And bring my damn check."

"Yes, ma'am."

On the line, I heard something that sounded suspiciously like a purr.

"Angela, tell me that's not you."

"Oh," she said, "that's Spanky. He came home to mama last night. This cat's working on his ninth life for sure."

After I hung up, I realized I might be working on an extra life myself.

22

You never know when things are going to turn around. That's why you shouldn't kill yourself. It felt great to be back in the gym with Angela, even though my first hour of practice was beyond pathetic. Still, to paraphrase those fishing T-shirts, "The worst day at the gym is better than the best day at the office."

It was an unbelievable start to the week. So far, Pam hadn't found out about my final check or how close I came to losing Angela. Two bullets dodged, possibly for good. How many more were left in the gun? I put the thought out of my mind and focused on the realization that I felt looser and freer than I had in days, like switching from briefs to boxers. The best part was, it carried over to my workouts. By Tuesday, I was showing steady improvement. On Wednesday, my three-point rate was close to sixty-five percent. Not coincidentally, my confidence was growing, too. Angela said she could see it in my eyes. More and more, I expected to make the shot. When everything clicked into place like the tumblers in a combination lock, my movements were fluid, even effortless. At those times, I felt as if I could shoot forever.

Unfortunately, my elbow had other ideas. On Thursday morning, I awoke to a dull throbbing pain. Testing the joint tentatively, I winced. It was telling me, in no uncertain terms, it needed a day off.

"Shit," I said.

"What's wrong?" Pam asked.

"My elbow's really sore. I'd better ice it down."

"You just lie there. I'll get the pack."

"I should call Angela. What'd I do with her phone number?"

"I don't know," Pam said. "Where did you see it last?"

"If I knew that, I wouldn't be asking, would I?"

"Aren't we cranky. I'll get some ice for your head, too."

After an hour or so, my elbow was making a minor comeback. Since we never found Angela's number, I decided to drive to the rec center to tell her in person.

"Sounds like a mild case of tendonitis," she said.

"What should I do?"

"Ice, aspirin, rest, and hope for the best."

"Thanks, Doc."

"And barbecue," she added. "Let's sneak out and get that lunch I owe you. I'll drive. You just rest that arm."

"Isn't it a little early for lunch?"

"It's never too early for Fat Daddy's."

"That's a great slogan. You should go into advertising."

I called Pam to tell her I'd be late and we were off in Angela's Olds. The vehicle had that distinctive musty-dusty old-car smell. The dash was festooned with a web of fissures and cracks, the work, possibly, of some schizophrenic spider. The front seat oozed foam rubber. When I slammed the passenger door, the window rattled.

"Not so hard," Angela cautioned. "Be sure and push the lock down. The door's been known to fly open."

"That's comforting," I said, reaching for the seat belt. Some kind of gunk in the mechanism made it difficult to buckle. It took three tries before the familiar "click" told me I was strapped in.

Angela said, "I haven't had a passenger in a while. If you can't get out of that belt, I'll bring you a doggie bag."

We chugged onto the freeway, belching black smoke, and headed downtown. Angela slid a tape into the deck.

High-pitched crackling and static filled the air. Without warning, she slapped the dash with her right hand. (That would explain the cracks, at any rate.) If I hadn't been strapped in, I would've jumped a foot off the seat. Instantly, the static was replaced by the unmistakable sounds of Nat Cole's "Route 66."

"Aren't you too young for this?" I asked. "Hell, I'm too young for it."

"I'm a third-generation fan. All the old-timers. Ella, Sarah, Joe Williams. My grandma got my mama hooked and she passed it down to me. When I was a little girl, I can remember the two of them putting on those old forty-fives and dancing around the kitchen. It makes me feel …" she searched for the right word, "… connected."

"Tell me about your family," I said. "You really miss them, don't you?"

"You know it. My daddy just retired from GM. From what I hear, Mama's tired of him already, hanging around the house, getting underfoot. She's been checking out the want ads for a part-time job."

"For him or for her?"

"Either one. As long as it gets one of them out of the house."

"Any brothers or sisters?"

"One of each. I'm the youngest by ten years. I think I was an accident, but my folks never let on."

"Are they excited about your new coaching career?"

"Well, I haven't told them, exactly. They weren't overly thrilled about me moving out here in the first place. If they knew I lost my job, I'd never hear the end of it. You know how parents are."

"I do. You're lucky, though," I told her. "Mine are both dead."

"Sorry."

"That's what happens when you get older. My dad just died a few years ago. He was in his eighties. Outlived all his family, friends, contemporaries. It must be a

weird feeling to be the last one left. There's nobody to
say to 'Remember when we did such and such?'"

"I can't imagine life without my folks," Angela said
quietly.

"You never get over it, but the pain dulls. After a
while, the memories become sort of bittersweet. You find
yourself smiling at some old picture or memento. The
other thing is, it makes you aware of your own
mortality. I'm in the batter's box now. There's nobody
between me and the ol' Grim Reaper."

"That'll straighten out your priorities, I'm guessing."

"You re-evaluate everything, try to figure out if you're
using your time wisely. Even if I hadn't won this contest,
I'd have quit my job eventually."

"And do what?"

"I'm not sure. Do you need an assistant coach?"

"There's no money in it."

"Maybe I won't need any."

Angela exited the freeway at Eastern Avenue and
turned right. We were going into a part of town that made
me thankful the doors were locked. On every corner, it
seemed, two or three black or Hispanic men congregated,
talking amongst themselves. Street people pushed shopping carts laden with big green trash bags or simply
shuffled along, muttering or screaming obscenities. I noticed that every strip mall had at least one boarded up
store or going-out-of-business sign. It was hard to believe
there was so much poverty in the shadows of a city de-
voted to the almighty dollar. We might as well have been
on another planet. I've often thought that we're all about
three or four bad breaks away from being homeless. A
regular Joe loses his job, his wife leaves him, he develops
a drinking problem, gets behind in his mortgage pay-
ments, the cold gray men from the bank take his house
back. Then, *zing*, something in his head snaps like an old
rubber band and he's taking up residence in a Maytag
carton. Maybe that's the real reason we don't want to

deal with them. Too close to home. There but for the grace of God, and all that.

I said, "Nice neighborhood."

"Yeah, when the shooting starts, I can always use you as a human shield. That's why I brought you along."

Fat Daddy's neon sign was on, even though it was daytime. The sweet smoky aroma of barbecue spilled into the parking lot and made my mouth water like a Pavlovian pooch. When we walked through the faded wooden door, I had the impression it was the kind of place that used to have sawdust on the floors, before some government agency decided that's hazardous to our health. A friendly fat woman led us to our booth.

"Haven't seen you in a while, honey" she said to Angela, while giving me the once-over. "Where you been keeping yourself?"

"Just workin'," she said. "But that gets old. I need a shot of good old-fashioned home cookin'."

"Well, you've come to the right place. Enjoy yourselves. Alma will be with you in a minute."

"Thanks."

We slid onto the hard wooden benches of our booth.

"I should've brought my own pillow," I whined.

"Quit your bitchin'," Angela said. "When the food comes, you'll forget all about your bony butt."

I opened the menu. It had a big brown stain in the center of the page. Barbecue sauce, I hoped.

"What do you recommend?" I asked.

"Since the name of the restaurant is Fat Daddy's Chicken & Ribs, I'd suggest something in a chicken or rib."

"You're a big help."

"How about the Sampler Platter? You get barbecue chicken and spare ribs, fried catfish, corn bread, and two sides."

"Sold. You know, technically, Jews aren't supposed to eat pork, but I do anyway."

"What's wrong with pork?"

"In the old days, people didn't cook it long enough and it made them sick. I suppose the Jews got tired of dying, so they banned the stuff outright."

"Well, they cook it here for about a week."

"I'll be sure to tell the rabbi. Maybe this will be his new favorite place."

I studied my choice of sides. Smothered greens, macaroni and cheese, black-eyed peas, candied sweet potatoes, dirty rice, fried cabbage, fried okra, fried corn.

"These look healthy."

"Yeah. Not like all that tongue and dumpling balls and filthy fish you eat."

"What's dirty rice?"

"It's probably too advanced for you. Rice mixed with ground-up organ meats. That's what makes it dirty."

"I guess I'll stick to something more familiar."

I ordered the Sampler Platter with macaroni and cheese and green-bean casserole. Angela got some stuff I've never heard of and hope never to see again. The main ingredient was something called ham hocks. The service was attentive, my order huge and mouth-watering. The sauce was just the right combination of sweet and spicy, leaving a slow-burning residue that lingered for hours. The ribs were the best I've ever tasted, crispy on the outside, moist and tender on the inside. The meat literally fell off the bones. Although it was still late morning, the place was filling up fast. An eclectic mix of locals, professionals in business suits, bikers, soccer moms, retirees, and scrounges still mourning the death of Jerry Garcia. All brought together by rib power, the real key to world peace.

While we worked on our meals, the conversation turned to, of all things, basketball.

"So, am I making progress?" I asked.

"Better than I expected. You must have a good coach." Angela looked pleased with herself.

"What am I, chopped liver?"

"You are merely the medium through which my genius is expressed."

"Oh, brother."

She chuckled. "Had you going for a second, didn't I?"

"Nah."

"Still, it shows the techniques work. I'm starting to believe anybody can improve."

"Even a guy like me. Here's a news flash. I'm gonna make that shot." I surprised myself by saying it.

"See, now you got attitude. That was the missing piece of the puzzle. Just keep thinking like that. Next week, we'll tie up some loose ends and you'll be good to go."

"I just thought of something," I said. "You're coming to Phoenix with us, right?"

"Hadn't really given it much thought."

"Give it some thought," I said, trying not to sound desperate. "It would mean a lot to me."

"All expenses paid?"

"Of course." More money I didn't have, but it would be worth it.

Angela popped a last morsel of fried something into her mouth, leaned back, patted her stomach gently, and said, "I'm there."

23

On Friday, two important things happened. My elbow felt better. And I got a chance to put my new attitude to the test.

As I've said, we normally had the gym to ourselves during the morning hours. Today was different. About a half-hour into our practice, two teenage boys walked in. They looked to be about sixteen or seventeen, heavily pierced and tattooed, both over six feet tall. Whether because of better nutrition or some new evolutionary enhancement, this generation was considerably larger than my own. What happened to all the short kids, I wondered. Who got picked last in gym class?

One of the boys was completely bald, except for a wispy red ponytail. The other appeared to be wearing a spiky sea urchin that someone had dyed yellow and plopped on his head. The bald kid had on a black T-shirt that said "No Fear," while his buddy's red tank top bragged "Big Johnson." A babe magnet, no doubt. They may as well have worn shirts that said "Future Ex-Cons." Both wore the longest baggiest shorts I'd ever seen. The term *shorts* was a misnomer, actually. More like trousers left in the dryer too long. You could see, maybe, two inches of ankle. Obviously, these boys shoplifted from the same store. If Amy ever brought either one over to the house, I'd have to lock her in her room for a year.

As they approached, No Fear said, "Hey, old dude." It took a moment to realize he was talking to me. Standing there with that smug teenage boy look on his face, he took a last drag on his cigarette and crushed it with his foot, right into the gym floor. The trouble with smoking, I've decided, is it doesn't kill people fast enough.

"Shouldn't you boys be in school?" I asked, playing the father role to the hilt.

"Nah," Big Johnson laughed. "Today's test day."

"And the tests are for everyone else?"

No Fear ignored my snappy comeback and asked, "You wanna run with us?"

For an instant I thought, *maybe these kids aren't so bad after all.* Softening, I said, "No thanks. I've gotta practice. Maybe we can run later."

As they both stared in confusion, Angela came up behind me and whispered, "No, Nick. They mean, do we want to play basketball with them."

"Oh," I said stupidly. "What do you think?"

"Let's pass. What if you get hurt?"

"You're right." Facing the boys, I said, "We appreciate the offer, but my coach here says I have to keep working."

They stared at Angela. "That sucks," No Fear said. "We don't have a game ball."

"Not our problem," Angela said, turning her back on them.

Under his breath, Big Johnson muttered, "Bitch."

Angela stopped in her tracks and spun to face them, her eyes flashing. "What did you call me?" she spat angrily.

Suddenly, the boys appeared to lose some of their swagger. "Nothing," Big Johnson said.

True to his name, No Fear refused to back down "You heard him."

"Shut up," Big Johnson said to his pal.

"Yeah, I heard him all right," Angela said. "Now you chumps listen to me. This is *our* house. Nobody comes in here and disrespects us in our house, you got that?"

They laughed nervously. "Yeah."

"You want a piece of me? Okay, how much money you got?" Angela asked.

No Fear said, "I don't know. Why?"

"Cause we're gonna take you boys to school. Old school. But I don't work for free. Let's see that chedda." As Angela spoke, her head seemed to bob and weave in time to the words, seemingly independent from the rest of her body.

They reached in their pockets and pulled out some crumpled bills and assorted change. It looked like just under seven dollars.

Angela counted it and said, "That'll work. Pay attention. We're playing to eleven by ones. Make it, take it. Win by two. I'll break."

It sounded like gibberish to me, but the boys nodded their heads. Panicked, I took Angela aside and said, "Wait a minute. What about me getting hurt?"

"Don't worry about it," she said icily. This was a different Angela, the one with her game face on. Her eyes took on the intense shiny look of a predatory animal.

"You were worried about it a minute ago."

"Here's the deal. I'm gonna smoke these punks. They can't handle me one on one. I'll take 'em to the rack all day. When they finally figure it out and I draw the double-team, I'll kick the ball out to you. Just hang around somewhere near the free throw line. If you're open, don't hesitate, just put it up. It'll go in."

"Okay," I said reluctantly. My mouth felt cottony and dry.

Angela put her hand on my shoulder. "You won't get hurt, I promise," she said. "I got your back."

"I'm more worried about my front."

She fixed the boys with a steely glare. "Let's ball."

Angela stepped up to the three-point line and calmly iced her shot. "It's ours," she said, flipping me the ball. "Take it out." Game on.

I in-bounded to Angela, with No Fear covering. She dribbled once, twice, gave him a nifty little crossover move that faked him out of those stupid shorts, then went strong to the hoop for an easy lay-up. She may not have had the quicks for the pro game, but she had more than enough for these boys.

"One zip," Angela announced, passing me the ball. Again, I brought it in. No Fear gambled and went for the steal, missing by inches.

"My bad," he apologized to his friend, but it was too late. Angela left him in the dust. She made a burst to the basket and, as Big Johnson converged to help out, switched the ball to her left hand and kissed it off the glass.

"Two zip," she said.

On our next possession, Angela took the ball off the dribble, stopping and popping for a sweet fifteen-footer. "Three zip," she crowed. "I'm feelin' it all the way!"

"Cover her!" Big Johnson yelled at his buddy.

"I'm trying, dickhead!" No Fear shot back. "You think you can do better, go for it."

They switched off. Angela backed her man into the low post and beat him with the sweetest junior skyhook this side of Magic Johnson. This wasn't just school, this was postgraduate work. They switched back.

"Four zip," Angela laughed. "You girls gettin' nervous?"

"Bring it," No Fear said defiantly. He sounded more confident than he looked.

This time, it dawned on the boys to double-team Angela. As advertised, she swung the ball out to me, wide open at the free throw line. Automatically, I put it up. Nothin' but net. I let out a little whoop, more out of surprise than anything else.

"Ooohh," Big Johnson said, not entirely sarcastically. Another indelible moment in my fledgling basketball career. One I would no doubt take to the grave.

"Five zip," Angela announced. "In case you lost track."

"We know the count," No Fear said angrily.

I grinned like a fool. Angela wasn't only a world-class athlete; she was a trash-talker extraordinaire.

Unfortunately, I got careless on my next inbounds pass and saw it picked off by No Fear, who overshot the ball so hard it banked off the backboard right into the hole.

"That's one," he said.

"The *only* one," Angela said. "Must be your birthday, 'cause that's a gift."

"Sorry," I told her.

"No problems. Just cover your man," she said, indicating Big Johnson, who was bringing the ball in. No Fear took the pass, dribbled, tried to make his move, but ran directly into Angela's well-placed hip, sending him sprawling to the floor.

"Foul!" he screamed, popping back up. His left knee had an angry red scrape that was beginning to drip blood.

Calmly, Angela said, "I don't think so, but take it up top. Your ball."

Still pissed, No Fear hit Big Johnson with a high, hard pass that caromed off his chest, right toward me at the three-point line. Scooping up the ball, I could hear Angela yell, "Shoot, Nick!" I knew it was good as soon as it left my hand.

"Six-one," I said, getting into the act.

"We got it goin' on!"

"Who's covering that guy?" No Fear asked.

Big Johnson said, "I thought *you* were."

"You gotta stick 'em," he said.

"Shut the fuck up. Who made you coach?"

The sounds of teamwork and good sportsmanship. Music to my ears.

Caught up in the moment, perhaps feeling a bit overconfident, Angela decided to bring the ball in. I dribbled clumsily and Big Johnson immediately stole it, taking it all the way.

"Six-two," he said.

On his next inbounds play, I got even, stepping in front of the ball and tipping it in Angela's direction. She drained a beautiful twenty-foot baseline jumper.

"Show us some love!" she sang. "Seven-two."

I was back to taking it out, so as not to handle the ball any more than necessary. Angela somehow got free of her man, and I hit her with a lob just over the outstretched arms of No Fear, now hopelessly out of position. Another easy bucket.

"Eight-two. You can quit anytime."

No Fear just glared at her. He might have been ready to cry.

On our next possession, Angela followed a rare miss with a perfectly timed offensive board for a quick put-back.

"Nine-two," she panted a little. "That cash is burnin' a hole in my pocket."

Again, I brought the ball in, but Angela got trapped in the corner by the double-team. She bounce-passed the ball to me, right through No Fear's legs, and I buried it as Big Johnson came flying in from the left side, too late.

"Money!" Angela said. "That's your new name, Nick."

I liked the sound of that. After all, I was three for three, with a steal and a shitload of assists, in case you're keeping score at home. We won't talk about the turnover.

"Yeah, I'm pretty fly for a white guy," I told Big Johnson.

He shook his head and said, "You're crazy." Which I probably was.

Unfortunately, what the basketball gods giveth, they taketh away. On my next try, I missed badly. No Fear grabbed the rebound and cleared it to Big Johnson, who went around me like I was glued to the floor, laying it up and in.

"Yo, Dawg, nice move," No Fear complimented his buddy.

"Ten-three," Angela said, "Don't miss now, or it's over."

No Fear didn't follow her advice. He took an ill-advised shot from way downtown, watching in disbelief as it bounced up and over the backboard. Our ball. Not taking any chances, Angela juked her man and sank a little five-foot runner. Eleven-three, your final score.

Angela and I made a big production of splitting our winnings, while the boys blamed each other for the debacle. It was the best $3.47 I ever made.

"It's a pleasure doing business with you," Angela called out. "Anytime you feel like losing to an old dude and a bitch, you pay us a visit. Just make sure you come correct."

"And pick up your damn cigarette butt on the way out," I added for good measure.

No Fear presented his middle finger for all to see, then they departed without a word.

Angela gave me a high five. "That's what I'm talkin' about, Money. Attitude. Every time you step foot on the court, you gotta believe you're the baddest motherfucker that ever laced 'em up. You got it?"

"I love it when you talk like that."

Angela smiled. "Damn. I'd almost forgotten what it feels like to kick some ass."

24

Her name wasn't Heidi, it was Kristie. And we were meeting at Starbucks at two o'clock. On my way out of the gym, she had smiled at me from behind the front counter and said, "You looked great out there, Nick."

Feeling myself turn crimson, I sputtered, "You were watching?"

"Absolutely. I wanted to see you teach those boys a lesson. They're such losers."

Jabbering on, I said, "I really didn't do anything. It was all Angela. I just stood around and let her feed me the ball. Of course, I did make a few shots, but ..."

"You're cute," she interrupted. "How about that cup of coffee? I'm off in a half-hour."

I gulped.

I gulped again.

I tried to keep my eyes from going wide, but in the process scrunched up my face till I was sure I looked like something smelled bad.

The silence was growing uncomfortable, unless you counted my runaway heart, which must have sounded like a bass drum.

Finally, when I managed to think of *something*, the best I could croak was, "I'm all sweaty."

"Doesn't bother me a bit."

Now I was ten minutes early, waiting for my Venti iced tea. At Starbucks, words don't have the same meaning as in the outside world. *Venti* is large, *Grande* is medium, and *Tall* is small. It's like George Orwell is in charge of the marketing department. I'm not a regular customer, so I can never remember which size is which. Invariably, my server will explain it in a slow condescending manner, looking at me with a mixture of pity and contempt, as if to say, "no one in the world could possibly be uninformed about our cup sizes." I'm not even bothered by it anymore; a good thing, because I know it will only get worse.

I parked myself near the creamer section and let my mind roam. What was Kristie's interest in me? I was flattered and more than a little curious. It couldn't possibly be my athletic ability, such as it was. Maybe she had a thing for older men. This would be a good way to test my value on the open market. At the agency, I'd had plenty of business lunches with attractive female clients, including a former first-runner-up in the Miss Nevada pageant. But nobody who looked like Heidi Klum. For just an instant, I pictured us living together in a Manhattan loft, sharing strawberry waffles and the *New York Times* in bed on a rainy Sunday morning, Kristie in nothing but my pajama tops.

Despite my erotic daydream, I knew I could never cheat on Pam. It just didn't jibe with the image I had of myself. Besides, there was too much history and friendship and yes, love, to throw it away on a fling. But if I knew my wife, she'd consider this cheating, anyway. Women are funny that way. For them, it's all about intent, while for men it's about action. Starting with a certain ex-president, we tend to be less picky about these things.

Kristie was right on time, looking amazing in simple white warm-ups. When she gave me a hug, she smelled like vanilla and fresh air. The fragrance of youth. I can't imagine what I smelled like. Old age and death, most likely. I had tried to clean myself up at the bathroom sink, but all I succeeded in doing was splashing water on my shirt and pissing off the guy who kept banging on the door.

Kristie ordered a Vente Mocha Frappaccino with a double shot.

"A double shot of what?" I asked.

"Espresso. I'm going out tonight and I need to stay awake."

I felt a sudden unexpected stab of jealousy. How stupid, I thought. Of course, a beautiful young girl is going out. What would you expect her to do, stay home and watch "Wheel of Fortune"? No, that was *my* gig. Besides, you don't even know her. And oh, by the way, you're married and old enough to be her dad. What the hell was I doing here, anyway? The jealousy quickly turned to guilt. I stuffed it down into its dark little hole, consoling myself with the thought, "It's just Starbucks. Not the Starbright Motel." So why were my palms sweating like a schoolboy at his first dance?

We claimed our drinks and settled into two upright chairs grouped together near the rear of the store. Self-consciously, I glanced around; with my luck, I'd run into a friend of my wife's and, to paraphrase Ricky Ricardo, "I'd have some 'splainin' to do." Fortunately, at this time of the afternoon, we had the place to ourselves.

"I'm glad you could meet me," Kristie said. Like a goddess mingling with mortals, she seemed to radiate light.

"My pleasure," I said, trying to sound cool. I hoped I wasn't staring.

"You're staring," she said brightly. Her eyes sparkled with amusement.

"Sorry. I zone out occasionally. It's these small seizures."

She laughed and ran a hand through her shimmering blonde hair. "I don't believe that for a minute."

I thought, there's nothing better than a gorgeous girl who laughs at your jokes. Pam's heard mine so many times she finishes the punch lines. The old guy's still got it. Time to put those high-school insecurities out of their misery once and for all. Triumphantly, I took a big swig of tea. In horror, I felt a few drops trickle down my chin onto my shirt, joining up with the sweat stains already in attendance. That shirt was fast becoming a piece of performance art. Or non-performance, as the case may be.

Kristie was sipping her own drink and seemed not to notice. "I was wondering if I could ask your advice on something."

"Anything."

"Well," she said, hesitating. "You're a man ..."

"Last I checked."

"I need a man's opinion. I've been going out with this guy for three or four months now. Brad. I like him a lot ..."

I tried to keep smiling while my fantasies evaporated like dew on a Vegas summer morning.

"... but he's sending me mixed signals. Like, sometimes he'll take me to a romantic dinner at the top of the Stratosphere and be all sweet and considerate, then other times ..."

Her luscious lips were moving, but I could only make out some of the words, because my brain was busy reminding me that "there's no fool like an old fool" in a voice that sounded suspiciously like my dad's. Still, I knew I'd have to give Kristie some kind of helpful feedback, so I forced myself to concentrate.

"... he's all distant and moody and he says he needs to spend more time on his career and maybe we should just be friends and see other people. And I can't talk to my father or brothers about this, and you've got a lot of experience and I was hoping you could explain what goes on in guys' minds and how to figure out what they're really thinking and …"

"That's your problem right there," I said, putting on my Fatherly Advice Hat. It was much more comfortable than the Dirty Old Man Hat I'd been trying out.

"What do you mean?"

"You're giving guys way too much credit. We're simple creatures at heart. Not much going on beneath the surface. When we say we want to see other people, it means we want to see other people."

"Oh." A storm cloud darkened her face and I kicked myself for being so tactless.

"But hey, maybe that's just me."

She shook her head slowly. "No, I'm sure you're right."

"Well, I'm sorry I am."

"It's okay."

"How old is this boy, anyway?"

"Twenty-five."

"And how old are you?"

"I'll be twenty-one in three weeks."

"He's too young for you. Women mature much faster than men. In girl-years, he's only about fifteen."

Kristie's face regained its customary glow. "And I'm very mature for my age. Everybody says so."

"Everybody's right. You need a man in his late twenties. Someone who knows how to treat a remarkable young lady like you."

"You really think so?" she asked self-consciously. Her neck took on a vivid pink hue.

"No question about it. Also, a bit of unsolicited advice. When you tell him, 'Sure, good idea. Let's see other people,' if he's like most guys, he'll flip out. All of a sudden, he'll become real possessive. He might even ask you to marry him! It's an old story—boy meets girl, boy gets girl, boy doesn't want girl, girl leaves, boy wants girl back. So be careful how you play it."

"I knew you were the person to ask. I just had a hunch." She leaned forward and gave me a quick kiss on the cheek.

I felt my own face turn pink. "This boyfriend of yours. What'd you say his name is?"

"Brad."

"Brad's a moron."

I should know.

25

"You should have seen me out there," I told Pam. "I couldn't miss."

"I know, dear. You said that already."

"We sent those kids home with their tails between their legs. They didn't know what hit them."

"That's nice."

"Angela was unbelievable. I've never seen anything like her."

"Good for Angela."

We were having dinner at our favorite Italian restaurant, Bambino's, where the meals are huge and the prices are small. It's a little locals-only place right out of a movie set: red-and-white checkered table cloths, dust-covered plastic grapes hanging from the ceiling, a pastel mural of Southern Italy, probably painted by the owner's cousin. We've been going there so long, they actually know our names, like on "Cheers." I was just finishing the last of the calamari appetizer. Pam was just coming to the end of her considerable patience.

"So Angela yells, 'The next time you feel like losing your money to an old dude and a bitch, you come see us.' That one kid flipped us off. Incredible. Just incredible. You have no idea …"

"Nick," Pam sighed, "I do have some idea because this is the third time I've heard it, and we've only been here fifteen minutes."

"Sorry." Getting on Pam's nerves hadn't been my intention when I suggested going out for a nice quiet dinner.

"You might find this hard to believe, but I had a pretty spectacular day, too."

"That's great. You have my undivided attention." I leaned forward in my chair and locked my eyes onto hers.

"Well, you know how I've been working on that special wish for Jeremy Shaw, the kid with Hodgkin's disease. I mean, he wants a cruise for his whole family. That's not the easiest thing in the world to pull off. Most of our kids ask for a trip to Disneyland, or they want to meet a famous athlete ..."

"Like me." Try as I might, I couldn't make myself shut the hell up.

One corner of Pam's mouth turned down for an instant, then she continued, "So I've been working on this for weeks, and today I get a call from Festival Cruise Lines, and they're going for it. Seven days to the Mexican Riviera, all expenses paid, airfare, the whole nine yards. You should have heard Jeremy when I gave him the good news. That was one happy sixteen-year-old ..."

"Sixteen, huh? That's about how old those boys were today. They looked like refugees from 'Mad Max.' It sure felt great to ..."

Pam pushed away from the table and stood up, a scowl spreading across her face.

"Where are you going?" I asked, knowing I'd crossed the line.

"I'm not sure. Some place where I don't have to hear your constant yakking about basketball."

"Sit down, honey. Please. I won't say another word."

"This is ridiculous. You're like a little kid. I never thought I'd say it, but I can't wait for this nonsense to be over. I just want to get my husband back. And my regular life," she said, still standing.

"Only one week to go."

"One of us may not make it."

"Look, I'm zipping my mouth shut." I made the third-grade zipping motion for emphasis.

"You don't have to do that. Just talk about something else for a change," she said, sitting down.

"One last thing, I promise. Did I tell you Angela gave me a new nickname?" I can never leave well enough alone.

"That might be the only thing you left out."

"Wanna hear it?"

"Do I have a choice?"

"It's 'Money.'"

"Money?"

"You know, like money in the bank. Right on the money. Money."

"I've got a better one for you."

"What?"

"Asshole. You know, like my husband's an asshole. A total and complete asshole. Asshole."

I mulled it over. "It doesn't have the same ring."

"You'll get used to it."

We ate the rest of our meal in silence. I hate it when Pam's mad at me. Right after we got married, she'd get angry and wouldn't tell me why. She'd pout, giving me the silent treatment all night. When I asked her if something was wrong, she'd shake her head no and storm off to rattle some dishes and bang some drawers. Finally, after I'd pestered her for a few hours, she'd say, "If you don't know what you did, I'm not going to tell you. That's part of the problem." Finally, after more pleading and wheedling and cajoling, she'd tell me—only to have "what I did" turn out to be something in my astrological forecast: "Mild flirtation turns serious." As we've gotten older, she's grown less sensitive and I've become more perceptive. Now when she's pissed, at least I know the reason. And this, of course, was a no-brainer.

"Do you want dessert?" I asked cautiously. The silence was becoming unbearable.

"No."

"They've got spumoni, your favorite."

No comment.

"Look," I said. "I apologize. You're right and I'm wrong. I know I've never said that before, but that's just the way it is. No more basketball talk. I swear."

"It's not just you, Nick. It's this whole thing. I like our life the way it is. Or *was*. If you make the shot, it'll all change forever."

"Does it have to?

"Of course it does. Money has a way of doing that."

"I thought you wanted this more than I do. The list, the bed and breakfast, the new couch, a better college for Amy, your dreams."

"Sometimes I think it's better if they stay dreams."

"So what are you saying? Do you want me to miss?"

"I don't know what I want."

"We can always give the money to charity," I offered.

She considered it for a moment. "No, just make your basket. We'll deal with it."

"That's more like it," I said. "Because I'm not sure I can miss on purpose."

What I didn't tell Pam, what I couldn't tell her, was that part of me didn't want this to end. Ever. I was having too much fun. For the first time, I was good at something besides writing ad copy. What a revelation for a guy like me, who mainly lived in his own head. I liked everything about my improbable new life. The smell of the gym, the feel of the ball, the subtle improvements, the way my muscles ached at the end of the day. I would try to explain it to Pam some other time. For now, it was safer to hide behind this big dish of spumoni.

26

As my last week of practice began, I had the sense of time speeding up. It reminded me of a gas tank, where the first half takes forever to go down, and the second half disappears so fast it makes slurping sounds. Partly, it was the realization that, in six days, I'd be standing on a basketball court in front of 20,000 people, on national television, with a million dollars on the line. Before, it seemed like some far-off event. Now, it loomed so large it obliterated everything else in my consciousness. Attitude or not, just thinking about it made my stomach do back flips.

At the gym, we mainly worked on fine-tuning. My success rate now hovered at seventy percent, which, according to Angela, was perfectly acceptable, considering the amount of time we had left. "That's about as good as it's gonna get."

"Really?"

"Hey, Money, three out of four ain't bad. I like those odds."

We also scaled back our practice sessions for fear of putting undue strain on my elbow. Bungee jumping and two-on-two basketball notwithstanding, this was no time to take chances. Instead, I spent even more time with the little man in my head, who never got tired, never strained a muscle, and still never missed a shot. I was getting so good at conjuring him up, I was able to put his tiny butt to work even while going about my other activities.

As we finished our Monday practice, Angela took me

aside and said, "Money, something else I been meaning to tell you."

Warily, I said, "Yeah?" Was Clyde back in the picture? I couldn't handle any more surprises.

In a deadly serious tone, she said, "I don't want you getting busy between now and Saturday."

"That's it? Fine, I don't mind cutting back on my chores. Maybe I can get the girls to run some errands for me."

Angela gave me a confused look, then tossed her head back and howled with laughter.

"What's so damn funny?"

Trying to catch her breath, Angela wheezed, "Nick, you might be the whitest man I ever met. I'm talkin' 'bout hookin' up, hittin' it, gettin' your groove on."

With slowly dawning comprehension, I said, "You mean sex?"

"That's exactly what I mean."

"Did Pam put you up to this?"

"Listen to me. You have sex, you lose your edge. I know what I'm talkin' about. From personal experience."

"Too much information," I told her.

"*After* you drain your shot, you'll have a million reasons to break her off somethin' proper."

Despite the moratorium on nookie, things were really heating up on the home front. More than ever, the fucking phone never stopped ringing. Reporters, relatives, well-wishers, salespeople, con artists of every stripe all wanted a piece of the action. Out of desperation, we turned off the ringer and let the calls go directly to tape, which filled up rapidly and had to be purged three or four times a day. Occasionally, a message captured my attention and warranted a callback. Like Bigg Fizz's own

Trip Treadwell, who tried to reach me on Tuesday.

"Mr. Nichols," he said cheerfully when I returned his call. "So nice to hear from you. How are you feeling?"

"Fine."

"Excellent. I just wanted to touch base and confirm your travel arrangements. You and your party are booked on America West Flight 642, departing McCarran International Saturday morning at 10:45, arriving at Phoenix Sky Harbor at 11:55 am. Our man will be at the airport holding a sign. Just look for him and he'll do the rest. Any questions?"

"Sounds easy enough."

"I'm looking forward to meeting you and your family. Have a safe journey."

"Thank you."

We hung up. Trip Treadwell was, without a doubt, the most unfailingly pleasant person I'd ever dealt with. It made me wonder what kind of medication he was on.

Later that day, Jason checked in.

"Hey, bro, how's it hanging?"

"About two inches … from the floor." We snickered. Junior-high humor is still the best.

"You ready to go?"

"Ready as I'll ever be. You're coming, right?"

"Of course. I have to protect my investment." A long pause, then the sound of Jason clearing his throat. "Nick, I did something really dumb," he said in a ragged voice.

"Not you too."

Hesitantly, he continued, "I drove down to the South Bay this weekend, put the Beamer through its paces. Looked up some old buds still living on the Strand. They turned me on to an investment opportunity, a little hot dog stand a hundred feet from the beach. Moon Doggies. Great name, huh?"

"Sounds familiar," I said.

"I thought so, too, although I can't seem to place it. But it's exactly what I've been looking for."

I rubbed my eyes wearily. "Tell me you didn't ..."

"We all went in together."

Jesus, had everybody taken stupid pills lately? "How much?" I asked.

"Fifteen thousand and change. The down payment. That place is a real cash cow, been there forever. Owner's getting old and can't handle it anymore. A once-in-a-lifetime thing, you know?"

"Let me ask you something. What's your situation at work? Are they paying you on time?"

Another pause, and I had my answer.

"Can you get your money back?" I asked.

"It's non-refundable."

"What do you have left in savings?"

"Gas money, basically. But I might be coming into a nice chunk of change, remember?"

I remembered, all right. I also remembered that Jason was just taking my own advice. Sure, it was an impulsive, even foolish, move. But Jason was young and his job was probably hanging by a thread. Besides, hadn't I done the same thing when I walked out of Dunbar's for good?

"You know what? You're right," I said. "Go for it. No regrets."

Instantly, I could hear the vitality return to his voice. "So I'll see you guys in Phoenix. I'm staying at my folks'. They have a condo."

"Watch out for that speed trap outside of Kingman. It's their only source of revenue."

"I know, I've contributed before."

"Have a safe trip."

"Hey, Nick."

"What?"

"Thanks for understanding."

We hung up. Hey, if worse came to wurst, I could always hit him up for a free dog.

At least some of the other pieces were falling into place. For her part, Pam took it upon herself to start cooking healthy. I'm sure it was her way of showing support. No more artery-clogging red meats and cheeses until after the big event. For dinner on Tuesday, she served up a humongous white blob that looked like a cross between vanilla pudding and Play-Dough.

"Ta-da!" she said with a flourish.

"What in God's name is this?"

"Garlic Tofu. I cut the recipe out of today's paper."

Yet another reason to hate the *Post*.

She added, "It's really good for you. Pure protein."

Pure crap was more like it. But for once, I held my tongue. Pam was trying really hard and the last thing I wanted was to hurt her feelings by rejecting her peace offering. Besides, I seemed to have less and less room for negativity in my life. I scooped up an extra large helping while she beamed. It was a good thing Amy wasn't home. I could picture her running out of the room, screaming.

"Well?" Pam asked.

"It's really something." Not a lie, really. It *was* something. I just wasn't sure what. I hoped I was accumulating points on the giant cosmic scoreboard. Actually, the stuff wasn't as bad as it looked. Kind of chewy. The only thing missing was flavor.

"I was afraid you wouldn't like it."

"Like it? Are you kidding?"

"That's wonderful, because I've got more healthy recipes for the rest of the week."

"I can't wait," I said, trying not to look panicky. I was imagining plates overflowing with bulgur wheat and veggie burgers and sprouts. Sprouts are the worst. Furtively, I glanced around the room for Flash. He was nowhere to be seen. Where was that damn dog when you needed him?

Even Amy was trying to pitch in. On Wednesday morning, she presented me with a gift, a pair of sunglasses. The lenses were dark and small, no bigger than quarters.

"They're Oakleys," she assured me.

"Thank you, honey. They must have been expensive."

"That's okay, I got a raise at work."

"You did? When? Why didn't you tell us? I'm very proud of you."

I tried them on. Immediately, I was standing in the dark.

"How do they look?"

"Awesome. Be sure to wear them when they introduce you on TV."

"Can I take them off for my shot?"

"Do you have to?"

"Only if you want me to see."

On the way to the gym, I allowed myself the idea that things might turn out okay. In the past, that just meant I didn't understand what was going on. But, as they say on those investment commercials, "Past history is not an indicator of future performance." A fancy way of saying, "We're covering our ass. How about you?"

I switched on the radio and found the local sports station. It was in the middle of the Biff & Burt Show, a couple of no-talents who know less about sports than my daughter. Biff (or was it Burt?) has the world's worst voice, a hoarse gravelly gargle topped off with a New Jersey accent. His partner is one of those annoying radio creeps known as a "puker," a phony-baloney dime-a-dozen announcer with no vocal equivalent in real life. If you met a guy at a party who talked that way, you'd have to kill him. Worse yet, he pops his p's, so that every mention of *Pittsburgh* or *player* produces a sound like a small explosion. Normally, their sole purpose in life is to piss me off. Today, I found them mildly amusing.

Until they started talking about me. "Let's turn now to the Western Region Final on Sunday," Biff said, "where heavily favored Arizona takes on a surprising UCLA squad."

"That's right, Biff," Burt jumped in. "Even though the Wildcats have been playing lights-out the second half of the season, you've got to like those scrappy Bruins, paced by all-everything point guard Jamal Martinez."

"He's leading the conference with nine point three assists per game, Burt."

"It's amazing how you come up with these stats right off the top of your head, Biff. Ha ha."

"I've got a mind like a steel trap, Burt. Ha ha."

"I thought that was a *mouth* like a steel trap, Biff. Ha-ha."

My attention began to wander until I heard one of them say, "And to add to the excitement, the halftime show will feature fellow Las Vegan Alan Nichols, the winner of the Bigg Fizz Million Dollar Challenge."

"You are correct, sir. That lucky so-and-so gets to shoot a three-pointer for a million bucks. Have you ever won anything, Burt?"

"Just a gift certificate for a prostate exam. Ha ha."

"Ouch. So what have you heard about this guy? Do you like his chances?"

"I saw him on the news a few weeks back. He stunk up the place."

"Figures. Why do the stiffs get all the breaks?"

"You think Bigg Fizz wants to part with a million bucks? I've lived in Vegas long enough to know the fix is in, my friend. The fix is in. I'm surprised they didn't pick the little old lady from Pasadena. Ha ha."

This was more than I could take. I whipped the car into the first parking lot on the right and headed for the nearest available pay phone. Fuming, fumbling for change, cursing myself for tossing my cell phone, I rifled through the telephone book until I found the radio station hotline.

"K-Sports," a perky female voice answered.

"Is this the 'Biff and Barf Show'?" I asked.

"Biff and Burt, yes."

"This is Alan Nichols. They were just talking about me. I need to speak to them."

"I'll be right back."

She put me on hold just in time to hear a spot for the ninety-nine-cent midnight breakfast special at the Lucky Charm Casino.

Soon, a familiar growl came on the line. "Biff Martin. Who's this?"

"Alan Nichols. The stiff who can't buy a shot."

"Hang on. We'll be back on the air in fifteen seconds."

Through the receiver, I heard Biff say, "Well, you never know who might be listening to the old 'Biff & Burt Show'. On the line right now is none other than Alan Nichols. Mr. Nichols, we were just talking about you."

"I heard."

"What can we do for you today?"

"I want to set the record straight. I quit my job, hired a coach, I've been spending the last three weeks at the gym, and I'm hitting seventy percent from the three-point line."

"Very impressive."

"Yeah, you can't trust TV reporters. Or radio doofuses, for that matter."

"Burt, I think we've been insulted."

"We've been called worse."

"So, are you making any predictions, Mr. Nichols?"

"Yeah, it's in the bag."

"You sound very confident."

"Here's how confident I am. What do you say we make a little side wager?"

Burt chuckled. "I'm not sure the casinos would like us cutting into their action. The last thing I need is some guy named Guido or Nunzio paying me the midnight visit, if you know what I mean."

"Well," I said, "what if we bet something other than money? My lawn could use mowing."

"And what do we get if you miss? Or should I say, *when* you miss."

"Name it."

"I don't know about you, Burt, but I could use a day off."

"Same here."

"Okay, Nichols, here's the bet. If the ball goes in, we mow your lawn. If it doesn't, you do our show for us. What do you say?"

"I say you'd better gas up the riding mower."

"We don't have a riding mower," Burt said.

"Too bad. I live on a third of an acre."

What a knucklehead you are, I told myself after hanging up. But all the way to the gym, I couldn't stop smiling.

27

After our Thursday workout, Angela said to me, "Don't show up tomorrow until about 11:30."

"How come?"

"It's a surprise."

"I hate surprises. What kind of surprise?"

"If I told you that," Angela said, "it wouldn't be a surprise, now would it."

"You can't argue with that logic."

All that afternoon, I tried to forget about the surprise, but my mind kept going back to it, the way your tongue keeps picking at a chipped molar. Over dinner, I said to Pam, "Angela's planning a surprise for me."

"I know."

"You do? I'm surprised."

"See, it's working already."

"So, what is it?"

"Angela swore me to secrecy."

"Since when did that ever stop you?"

"Since now."

"Tell me one thing. Am I gonna like it?"

"Of course."

"Are you gonna be there?"

"That's two things."

"Just tell me."

"Maybe."

I pushed my chair away from the table and stood up, saying, "You're driving me crazy."

Pam said, "It's not a drive. It's more like a short walk."

Friday morning, 11:25. The rec center parking lot seemed unusually full. Maybe it was for one of those Mommy and Me classes in the back room, or Senior Water Aerobics out by the pool.

As soon as I entered the building, Kristie greeted me with a big smile. "Hi, Nick. Thanks again for the advice the other day. It really helped."

"Any time. Hey, what's with all the cars out there?"

"You'll see. Go right in."

"Is everybody in on this?"

"Basically."

Despite my best efforts, my heart gave a little skip. I pushed the door open and stepped into the gym. I've been in caves that were brighter. Before my eyes had a chance to adjust, somebody hit a switch and flooded the room with light. Blinking, the first person I noticed was Angela, bouncing a basketball in the middle of the floor. Her smile was as brilliant as the spotlight. The next thing I noticed was the bleachers. They were full. A couple of hundred people, at least. As one, they began stomping and clapping, taking up a rhythmic chant of "Nick! Nick! Nick!" Strangely embarrassed, I gave them an awkward little wave as I made my way toward Angela.

"Who are these people?"

"Your fans, Nick."

"Where'd they come from?"

"Everywhere. Salvation Army, Midnight Mission, Fremont Street. All I had to do was make a few calls."

"It must have cost you a fortune."

"Nah. They work for food."

"Seriously? People do that?"

"Sure, if they're hungry."

"What kind of food?"

"Pizza. I had a coupon."

"I don't know what to say."

"That's a first."

I gave her a hug instead. Now it was Angela's turn to be flustered.

"You just get your ass over to that line and start putting up shots. Let's see how you do in an actual simulated pressure situation."

I did as I was told, amidst a chorus of cheers, whistles, and applause. "So this is what it's going to be like," I said to myself. "Times a thousand."

I took my first shot. It missed. After a brief moment of silence, the boos started, building to a climax not unlike a flock of angry owls. "How quickly they turn," I thought. They were really into their roles now. Angela had prepped them well.

My second shot was closer. It appeared to be on the way before rattling out. The crowd let loose with a long disappointed "Ooooohhhhh!" At least they were pulling for me. Okay, enough was enough. Time to settle down and give them their money's worth. *Bang*. Knocked it down. The place erupted in a thunderous roar. Chalk up another timeless image for the mental scrapbook.

Now I was in the zone. Five, six, seven, eight straight. Each time, I was greeted by the same outpouring of sound. If anything, even noisier than before. As I sunk my ninth in a row, I thought I could hear music coming from somewhere, possibly the gym's PA system, or maybe it was all in my head. Low at first, then growing louder and louder, until the now unmistakable horns blared through the gym and echoed off the walls. Of course. The theme from "Rocky." The corny over-the-top feel-good soundtrack for an entire generation. Instinctively, I raised my hands over my head and danced victoriously around the floor. Maybe they'd erect a statue in my honor at the top of the rec-center steps. Unexpect-

edly, somebody cut the main switch, bathing me in the
spotlight glow. Squinting, I looked across the gym to see
a figure running in my direction. Pam. She threw her arms
around me as the music reached its crescendo. "I'm so
proud of you," she kept saying. I'm not sure, but I might
have called her Adrian.

28

I came *this* close to getting away clean.

After Angela's extraordinary off-off-off Broadway production, I went home to think and focus, while Pam stopped at the store to pick up some last-minute provisions. I never have to worry about traveling, thanks to my wife's remarkable logistical skills. Packing, boarding the dog, canceling the paper, notifying the post office, it's all handled. I'm on a need-to-know basis. All I have to do is show up at the appointed hour and be ready to go. Oh, and make sure all the electrical devices are turned off. A couple of years ago, we returned from a weeklong beach vacation to discover that Amy had left the curling iron on. A good thing it wasn't next to a roll of toilet paper, or we'd have spent plenty of quality time with the Good Hands people.

As I was downing the last of my post-celebration beer, the sound of our creaky front door reminded me for the umpteenth time to break out the WD-40. *Who am I kidding*, I thought. Besides, I find the noise oddly comforting, sort of a low-tech early-warning system. Today, it wouldn't be warning enough.

My heart bounced joyfully when Pam entered the den. I was still on a high from earlier in the day. "Hi, babe. Need help with the shopping bags?"

Pam shook her head. "I don't have any."

Normally, that was enough to take me to yellow alert. But I was feeling too damned good to notice. Still, something wasn't quite right. "What do you mean? I thought you ..."

"Guess who I ran into at the checkout counter?"

A knot began slowly tightening around my gut, but I didn't know why. No question, my stomach is smarter than my brain. "Who?"

"Barbara Riley."

"Doesn't ring a bell."

"Sure it does. Tom Riley's wife, from work."

"Oh, right." For the life of me, I couldn't figure out where this was going, but it sure seemed important to Pam. "Is Tom okay?"

"He's fine." Pause. "Except he hasn't been paid in more than three weeks."

The knot pinched shut. "Oh," I managed to squeak.

"Dunbar's bankrupt."

My brain had exactly two seconds to come up with the perfect alibi and couldn't. "I know."

Pam's face was a stone mask right out of Easter Island. "How long have you known?"

"A couple of weeks, maybe. I was going to tell you."

"When?

"Soon. I didn't want you to worry." I stood up and took a step toward her. She took a step back.

"Did you ever get your final check?"

"No."

"Nick," she said in her chilliest tone, "when did we start keeping secrets from each other?"

"I'm sorry. I kept waiting for the right time and things kept cropping up and then I'd get distracted and forget about it for a while." I shrugged.

"How about when I bought the couch? You could have told me then."

"You were so happy, I didn't want to ruin it."

She folded her arms. "Ever since you quit your job, it's been one bad decision after another."

"I know, but that's over now. Just one more day," I

said in full salvage mode. "No matter what happens, we'll have enough money to get by."

"That's not the point. How can I ever trust you again?"

Flash, feeling the tension, backed out of the room. I wished I could follow him.

"Wait a minute," I heard myself scrambling, "I didn't *lie* to you."

"You withheld the truth. It's the same thing."

"No it isn't! I only didn't tell you so it wouldn't spoil your mood. Or mine. I really didn't want to think about it. Especially with a million bucks riding. And now my decision to leave Dunbar looks like pretty good foresight, I think."

I tried all my best rationales and logic. Nothing doing. Pam wasn't buying—groceries or any lines. I'd committed the mortal sin: not telling her something I knew, the nanosecond I knew it.

Finally, I held out my hands imploringly. "I'll make it up to you."

"I don't deserve this."

"You're right. Whatever you want, just say the word."

"It's too late for that."

"What do you mean?"

Cracks of sadness splintered her impassive features. "I'm not going."

"Pam, I can't do this without you!"

I felt my world unravel as she said, "You're going to have to."

29

On Saturday, we arrived at McCarran International Airport two hours early, me dragging my ass along with our luggage. I parked on Level 1M of the McCarran parking structure, a mammoth concrete spiral edifice that looks like a modern day version of the Colossus of Rhodes. When Amy was younger, she used to call it the "roller-coaster road." She'd scream, "Faster, faster, Daddy!" turning three shades of green while Pam yelled at me to slow down.

Level 1M is the Stardust Level. As far as I know, Las Vegas is the only city in the world that makes its parking levels available for corporate sponsorship. It's a bizarre application of our roaring capitalistic spirit, but it does help you remember where the hell you left your car.

McCarran itself is beautiful, an odd word to describe an airport, but appropriate nonetheless. In the mid-'90s our City Fathers decreed that Las Vegas's airport should be at least as attractive as the casinos themselves, especially because it was often visitors' first and last impression of our fair city. And so, a massive remodeling project remade McCarran into a gleaming futuristic transportation complex, replete with giant video screens running an endless loop of exquisitely filmed casino ads, a smooth silent network of trams to whisk passengers away to the outlying terminals, neon-wrapped glass elevators, and bank upon bank of shiny new slot machines. Not just any slot machines, but the worst-paying slot machines this side of any corrupt, tin pot, third world casino you choose. Unlike their hotel counterparts, these machines are eerily quiet, the first tip-off for the veteran gambler. The distinctive clank of money hitting the tray is so rare as to be positively jarring. Legend has it that many a traveler has squandered his or her entire bankroll before leaving the airport, only to turn around and board the next available plane out of town. Not exactly the best advertisement for repeat business, but Vegas has never been known for its long-term thinking. "What Happens Here Stays Here," is our official slogan. Starting with your money.

Squinting through bloodshot eyes, I checked the America West screen and learned that our flight was on time, departing from gate B-2. After a long line and a semi strip-search at the metal detectors, we found Angela waiting for us at the gate. She had positioned a book, carry-on bag, oversized purse, and cloth overcoat across an entire row of chairs. After we said our hellos, I asked, "Is this stuff all yours?"

"Uh-huh. I saved you some seats."

"Thanks. I guess you don't believe in traveling light."

"Hey, I don't believe in traveling at all. Especially if it involves airplanes. I'm what you call a white-knuckle flyer." She looked at her knuckles and laughed.

"This should be interesting."

"I almost called Jason and asked to drive down with him."

"Trust me, this is safer. You know, I thought you weren't afraid of anything."

"I never said that. I said we should all face our fears, and that's exactly what I'm doing."

"Well," I said, "I'm just happy you're here. And thanks again for yesterday. That was like something out of a movie."

Angela looked proud of herself, as well she should. "Just trying to give you that extra edge."

"I only have one complaint."

"What's that?"

"I never got any pizza."

She reached in her giant economy-sized purse and produced a triangular object wrapped in tinfoil. "I got you covered."

We briefly stood in line to get our seat assignments. Afterward, Amy wandered off to buy magazines, while Pam and Angela made plans to hit "Old Town Scottsdale," which I gathered had something to do with shopping. That's right, Pam had slept on it and changed her mind. I hadn't slept at all. Earlier that morning, when she told me she'd be joining us, I almost cried. But it didn't mean all was forgiven, not by a long shot.

"We still have plenty to talk about," she informed me. When that would happen was anybody's guess. At the moment, I was getting the silent treatment in spades. I didn't care. Pam was flying to Phoenix and that's all that mattered.

I flopped onto a chair, worked on my cold pizza and tried not to think too much about tomorrow. Just let it unfold on its own terms. Soon, a distorted voice told us it was time to board. With the price of airline tickets these days, you'd think they could pop for a better sound system.

"Where're you sitting?" I asked Angela.

"Front-row center."

"I'm impressed. I never knew anybody who was numero-uno before."

"I got a seat right up near the cockpit, so I can hear what's going on."

"Good idea. As soon as the crew starts putting on their parachutes, you'll be the first to know."

When the voice said it was our turn to board, we headed toward our seats in the second emergency row. I've always liked these, because they seem to give you more leg room.

Also, they're less claustrophobic. Instead of staring at the seatback in front of you, you get to stare at actual people. Sometimes they're even interesting. That's how I met the real-estate agent who sold us our house, as well as a developer who became a high-powered client for the ad agency, back when I cared about such things. Today, we sat across from a fresh-faced couple in their early twenties. They were very affectionate, sharing private snippets of conversation, the secret code of young lovers. Newlyweds, no doubt. Good. They weren't aware of anybody but themselves and I was in no mood for chitchat. Were Pam and I ever like that? I couldn't recall. I'd have to ask her sometime. She has a memory like a stenographer. She can repeat, word-for-word, a discussion we had in 1989. Not only can't I remember the discussion, I can't remember 1989.

I was plucked from my reflections by a minor disturbance in the front of the plane. The flight attendant, or server, or whatever they call them these days, was having trouble closing the overhead bin. I could hear Angela saying, "Be careful. Don't break anything."

"Ma'am," the attendant said, "I'm doing the best I can. You're lucky I don't make you check these items."

Angela might have mumbled something about taking the bus. With one last superhuman effort, the attendant shoved the stuff into the compartment, managing somehow to click it shut. If we were to hit choppy weather, I could foresee the bin flying open, flinging tinfoil-wrapped pizza and God knows what other emergency provisions throughout the cabin. The attendant, still out of breath, continued to make her way down the aisle, issuing the usual instructions about upright seats and tray tables, until stopping at our row.

"You *do* know you're in the emergency section, don't you?" she asked. She was a frumpy middle-aged woman, not at all like the airline personnel of yesteryear.

I almost didn't have the energy to be snippy, but still

managed, "Oh, is that what the sign means?" Pam gave me a "dummy up" look.

"Yes. In the unlikely event of an emergency, one of you has to be prepared to remove the door and assist with the evacuations."

"No problem," I said. "We were just in the process of electing a row monitor."

Our attendant favored us with a tight humorless smile. "Very good," she said. "But it can't be the young lady," she said, indicating Amy. "You have to be over eighteen."

"I *am* eighteen," Amy objected. "But don't worry. If this thing goes down, you're all on your own."

"See, we're on top of it," I said happily as she toddled past us.

"What a witch," Amy said.

"A regular ray of sunshine," Pam agreed.

"So who's in charge?" I asked, looking at the couple facing us.

The young woman said, "James just passed his test for the Phoenix Fire Department. You'll do it, won't you, James?" She gazed up at her husband proudly.

James appeared slightly embarrassed, but said, "Sure."

I said, "It's nice to know we've got a professional in our midst." I closed my eyes and tried to catch a few much-needed winks as the jet taxied down the runway and became airborne. I couldn't remember the last time I was so bone-numbingly fatigued.

Pam, however, felt like talking. Just not to me. She said to the couple, "So, you two live in Phoenix?"

"Yes," the woman said. "We're just coming back from our honeymoon. I teach second grade, and James is going to be a firefighter. Where are you guys from?"

"Las Vegas."

Her eyes widened. "People actually live there?"

"Sure, it's just like any other city, once you get past

the slot machines at the grocery store."

"I'm not sure I could handle it. Don't you gamble all the time?"

"It wears off really fast, after you figure out you can't win. Some people never get it and they have to move. Every now and then I'll throw some change in a video poker machine, but I can take it or leave it."

"Have you ever won?"

"Once I won a thousand dollars at the Speedee-Mart."

My eyes popped open. "You did? How come I'm just now hearing about it?"

Pam skipped only a beat before saying coldly, "I took you to Huey's for dinner and even slipped you a hundred."

"Oh, right."

Pam's good, I'll give her that. I had no idea if it really happened or if she was making it up. One thing's certain. If I ever get Alzheimer's, nobody will know the difference.

Again, I closed my eyes. A few minutes later, the young woman asked, "What brings you to Phoenix, business or pleasure?"

"Well, both, I guess," I heard Pam say. "My husband won a contest. He's going to shoot a basketball for a million dollars at tomorrow's game. Tell them, Nick."

James perked up and I heard him ask, "You're the Bigg Fizz guy?"

Shit, I thought. There goes my nap. Pam, skilled passive-aggressive that she is, was still getting even. "That's me."

"I played high school ball," James said.

"You don't say."

"He was very good," his wife informed us. "That's where I met him. He looked so cute in his little uniform."

James was blushing now. "Stop."

"Well it's true, you were the best-looking guy on the squad. My great big basketball hero."

I looked around for the airsickness bag, just in case.

"Good luck tomorrow," he said to me.

"Thanks. I'll need it."

"Can I make a suggestion?"

"Why not?"

I'm sure it was an excellent suggestion, but I never got to hear it. At that very moment, the bottom dropped out of our flight. The jet must have hit a downdraft, because it plummeted I don't know how many thousand feet, like a runaway elevator or some crazy middle-aged bungee jumper. I reached instinctively for Pam, who already had her arms around Amy, as a serving cart careened drunkenly about the cabin, throwing off bottles and cans like an out-of-control New Year's reveler. James was attempting to comfort his wife, now making soft whimpering noises. Above the din, the no-nonsense voice of the captain barked over the intercom, "Flight attendants, take your seats now!" In the first row, I could make out Angela's hand, gripping the armrest with every ounce of her considerable strength. I was sure her nails were leaving an impression for all time.

As quickly as it fell, the plane leveled off. An uneasy calm descended upon the cabin while we waited to see if another more precipitous dive was in the offing. I was grimly reminded of the old joke, "It's not the fall that kills you, it's those sudden fucking stops." As second after second ticked away, we could feel the tension begin to ease. A conversational buzz swept the plane, a happy byproduct of the realization that we were not going to die in a fiery crash after all. At least, not at that particular moment. Like most people, I've had my share of close calls. Like the time I plowed through a red light in a zero-visibility rainstorm, miraculously swerving to miss the dozen or so cars already in the intersection. I remember pulling over to the side of the road, sitting there trying to catch my breath and slow my machine-gun heart, wondering how I managed to avoid becoming road kill. (Not to mention taking out all those innocent victims.) I'm still not sure how I walked away from that one. In a parallel universe, I'm probably dead.

"Are you okay?" I asked my family.

"I think," Pam said.

"I spilled Coke on myself," Amy said. They both looked pale as chalk. I stretched my arm around both of them. Sometimes, that's the best you can do.

"I'm sorry," I whispered in Pam's ear. "About everything."

"Me too."

The weight lifting from my shoulders was enough to keep the plane aloft indefinitely.

Again, the P.A. sprang to life. The captain, less authoritative than before, said, "Sorry about that folks. Just some unexpected weather that didn't show up on the forecast. I don't think we'll have any more trouble between here and Phoenix, so just sit back and try to enjoy the rest of the flight. We're still on schedule and should begin our final descent in about twenty minutes." Our final descent. I wish he hadn't said it like that.

I looked at the young couple sitting across from us.

"Good job," I told James. "Thanks for not opening the emergency exit."

His wife stared at him with those moist puppy dog eyes. "That's my husband. He's so brave."

Thankfully, the remainder of our flight was smooth as Teflon-coated glass. Staring out the window, I was struck by the vast sprawl that is Phoenix. Like Las Vegas, Phoenix is one of the fastest growing cities in the country. It's a bigger sweatier version of Vegas, without the gambling to recommend it. It has more people, more heat, more swimming pools, more golf courses, more everything. Including this year's NCAA Western Region Finals, which might go a long way toward deciding the outcome of, oh, the rest of my life.

As if to make up for our unscheduled detour, the landing was barely noticeable. Ignoring the flight attendant's admonitions to remain buckled and seated until coming to a complete stop, everybody jumped up at once, eager to set foot on terra firma. Gathering up our belongings, we headed for the exit, only to find Angela still seated, still clutching the armrest, gazing blankly at the wall ahead.

Gently touching her shoulder, I said, "We're here. We can go now."

She jerked her head around, seeming to look right through me. "Huh?"

"We're on the ground. Let's get off this bucket of bolts."

One by one, she released her fingers from the armrest and rose shakily from her seat.

"Don't forget your stuff," I said. "Here, we'll help you."

By the time we collected her belongings, we were the last ones to, in airline-speak, deplane.

"That was the worst experience of my life," Angela told the flight attendant, now waiting impatiently for us to get the hell off her jet.

"We're very sorry. These things happen sometimes."

I looked at her and said, "I have to know. On a scale of one to ten, ten being Buddy Holly time, what was that?"

She thought for a moment before answering. "Oh, I'd say a six. I've definitely seen worse."

"Whatever they pay you," Pam said, "it's not enough."

"I agree," she said, smiling. "I hope the rest of your trip is more pleasant."

On the way out, I could hear her ask a co-worker, "Who's Buddy Holly?"

Heading down the ramp toward the gate, Angela, more herself now, said, "If you make your shot, I'm buying a new car and driving back to Vegas."

"What if I don't?"

She began to hum an old tune. Fats Domino, I think. Only later did I remember the words. "I'm walkin', yes indeed ..."

30

The first thing we noticed upon entering the concourse was a uniformed figure holding a hand-lettered sign reading "Nichols." He was tall, dark, and bore more than a passing resemblance to Billy Dee Williams in *Lady Sings the Blues.*

Angela said under her breath, "That is one fine-lookin' man."

"He's a hottie," Amy agreed.

Angela appeared to be undressing him with her eyes, until they came to rest on the name badge pinned directly over his chest pocket. It read "Clyde."

"I don't believe this," she muttered.

"What're the odds of that?" I wanted to know.

"I'm cursed."

We introduced ourselves to Clyde, who gathered up our carry-on bags and piled them onto a handcart.

"Did you check any luggage?" he asked.

"Yes," I said. "Our teenage daughter brought enough for a month."

"You can't be too careful," Amy said.

Clyde said, "Very good. Follow me to baggage claim." All business and corporate efficiency.

He led us to a moving walkway that was so long, we couldn't see the end. By the time we reached the carousel, it was just beginning to spit out our cargo. Within five minutes, we had collected a half-dozen assorted cases, hopefully ours, and our little caravan was again on the move. The baggage lady, recognizing Clyde, motioned us through the turnstile without stopping. No matter where you go, it pays to have juice.

Our stretch limo, a shiny black Lincoln, waited for us by the curb, its motor purring softly. As Clyde deftly fed our stuff into the maw of a bottomless trunk, Angela commented, "I could get used to this in a hurry."

"I know," said Amy. "Me too!"

Clyde opened the rear door, helping the women into the car's apartment-sized interior. At once, they began fiddling with the VCR, the CD player, the wet bar, the refrigerator, and the other gizmos. You'd think they were the Beverly Hillbillies, the way they were acting.

"No hot tub?" I joked.

"That's in the bigger limo," Clyde said. "We don't get much call for that this time of year. But help yourself to drinks. The bar is well-stocked with premium liquor."

Amy's face lit up.

"And soft drinks for the young lady," Clyde added.

"I hate being eighteen," she pouted.

"You'll appreciate it when you're my age," Pam said.

Amy sat back in her seat, crossed her arms, and sulked. I like it when she sulks. At least she's quiet.

"I hope you had a nice flight," Clyde said.

"We've had better," Angela replied.

"Well, it's smooth sailing from here. We'll be at your hotel shortly. Just press the intercom button if you need anything." I started to hit the switch to raise the partition, but Angela whispered for me to keep it open.

Clyde expertly guided the monster Lincoln through traffic, depositing us at the downtown Hyatt Regency in less than ten minutes. Amy and Angela were both disappointed.

"Can't we drive around some more?" Amy asked.

The Hyatt, a low-slung structure (by Vegas standards) with some kind of needle thing jutting up from the center, sits almost directly across from America West Arena.

That would certainly simplify things come tomorrow. No unpleasant mechanical breakdowns to worry about. We could just walk. What a concept. I was impressed with the folks at Bigg Fizz. They seemed to have thought of everything.

The Hyatt's space-age lobby looks like something designed by Stanley Kubrick, complete with a seven-or eight-story stark-white atrium and distinctive whooshing glass elevators. After dropping off our luggage, Clyde handed me a business card.

"If you're in need of transportation," he said, "you can contact me at this number. I'm on call twenty-four hours a day."

"We'll let you sleep, if at all possible," I said. I tried to toke him, as we say back home, but he politely refused, explaining, "It's covered." As Clyde pulled away from the curb, I thought I saw a wave of sadness wash across Angela's face. Despite the name.

"Nice guy," I said.

"Maybe you'd better let me hang onto that card," Angela said. "I wouldn't want you to lose it. Just in case we need a ride." I handed her the card and promptly forgot about Clyde.

Pam and Amy were already at the desk, checking us in.

"Ah, Nichols," the pasty middle-aged clerk said, fixating on his computer screen. "Nichols. I'm afraid I've got some bad news," he said dourly.

Shit, I thought. After the airplane incident, I couldn't wait to hear what this was all about.

The man continued, "There's been a slight, er, mixup. We've had to upgrade you to the Presidential Suite." He gave Pam a conspiratorial wink. "I hope you don't mind."

"We'll learn to live with it," she responded, with just the right officious tone.

As the bellman delivered us to our room, at the end

of the hall on the tenth floor, Amy whispered, "The Presidential Suite sounds good. Right?"

"Right," I said. "I guess the president's not staying here tonight."

His loss. The Presidential Suite was one of the nicest hotel rooms I've ever seen, and I've been around the block a time or two. There's nothing like walking through those heavy double doors for the first time, not knowing exactly what to expect. Pam let out a little gasp, Amy said "Wow," and Angela just stood there with her mouth open.

"Be cool," I whispered. "Act like you've been here before."

Slipping the bellman a Benjamin, just for the hell of it, I said in my best tweedy rich guy voice, "Thank you, my good man. That will suffice for now."

"Yes, sir," he said, his eyes bugging out. "Let me know if you need anything. Anything at all."

He deferentially backed out of the room, carefully closing the doors behind him. We stood in the foyer, surrounded by luggage, looking for all the world like a lost band of refugees.

"Well, let's get this stuff put away," I ordered, taking charge. "Don't just stand here with your thumbs up your …"

"Nick!" Pam cut me off. "Try to behave, just for the weekend. Promise?"

"Promise," I said, not wanting to be the cause of any more wifely cold shoulders.

The suite's living area was larger than the house I grew up in. It had a floor-to-ceiling solid-oak entertainment center, matching twelve-seat dining room table, full-sized kitchen, and an executive desk that would make Steve Wynn envious. Amy took off to explore the master bedroom, while Angela disappeared into the other bedroom to put her things away. Pam and I lingered in the middle of the suite, drinking in the surroundings, the lord and lady of the manor.

"Not bad," I said, wrapping my arm around her waist and drawing her closer.

She looked up at me and smiled.

Suddenly, Amy yelled from the bedroom, "Mom, Dad, come here! You've got to see this!"

We rushed in to find her sprawled across a gigantic four-poster bed, pointing to a wicker gift basket overflowing with fruit, cheese, crackers, chocolates, champagne, and the obligatory six-pack of Bigg Fizz.

"Three guesses who *that's* from," I said.

Pam said, "It's too bad the stuff's undrinkable. It makes me feel guilty."

"I know. It tastes like a cross between grapefruit juice and baby aspirin. But it makes you burp like a mother."

"As if you needed the help."

"So," Amy interrupted, "where are you guys sleeping tonight?"

"Right here," I said. "There's a big old sofa out there with your name on it."

"Dad," she whined. "That's not fair."

"Well, I guess you could always sleep in the tub."

A soft knock on the bedroom door ended that particular discussion.

"Can I come in?" Angela asked.

"Sure, it's open," Pam said, "How's your room?"

"It's bumpin'. Except there's a phone in the bathroom, right next to the toilet. Damndest thing I ever saw."

I said, "Remember, this is the Presidential Suite. That's probably where he conducts most of his important business."

Angela just shook her head. "Makes me sorry I voted for the man."

Speaking of telephones, the one on the nightstand was blinking. I picked it up and retrieved two voicemail messages. The first was from Jason McBride. He was briefly detained in some jerkwater town for driving one-ten in a twenty-five-mph zone, but would catch up with us later. Knowing Jason, he probably had the stereo cranked so loud, he couldn't hear the radar detector.

The second was from Trip Treadwell, who was taking us to dinner at the Compass, the revolving restaurant at the top of our hotel. Reservations were for seven. Since it was now only 12:35, we had some time to kill. Lunch and a nap sounded like just the ticket. Especially the nap.

31

"It's such a pleasure finally meeting you all," Trip Treadwell enthused. "It's always fun matching the voices to the people."

Pam, Amy, Angela, and I were sitting at a table in the Compass restaurant, sipping our drinks, watching Phoenix slowly revolve outside the big picture window. Treadwell was pretty much what I expected. A smooth-talking corporate type. Bland good looks, deeply tanned skin, perfect Tic-Tac teeth, a head full of thick brown hair. It's what I call "TV hair," the kind that never gets mussed in a wind storm or a tennis game, the kind that bounces back perfectly after a shower with just a few brush strokes or the merest shake of the head. The kind I never had, even as a kid. There isn't much I'm envious of, but I would kill for that hair.

Treadwell was probably in his late thirties, certainly younger than me. Lately, everybody was younger than me. Another fact of life I was still getting used to.

"I trust everything is to your liking," he continued. "The limousine service, the hotel, your suite."

"It's been great," I said. "Much more than we expected."

Treadwell smiled. "Excellent. We pride ourselves on our ability to get things done. You know, Bigg Fizz hasn't been on the market all that long, and we're anxious to take it to the next level. Compete with the giants of the industry, if you will. We think tomorrow's contest will go a long way toward giving us that kind of visibility."

"You won't hear us complaining," I said. "I'm glad to help."

"Mr. Stanley will be pleased to hear that."

"Mr. Stanley?"

"Harrison Stanley the Third. Our CEO. He'll be at the game tomorrow, presenting your check."

"I guess I'd better be nice to him."

"Everybody's nice to Mr. Stanley."

"I'm sure they are," I said. Some things never change. Stanley's toadies most likely had their noses so far up his ass, it smelled like Listerine to them.

The waiter, an all-American college boy, came to take our orders.

"My name is Justin and I'll be your server tonight."

"Hi, Justin," Pam said. Amy sat up a little straighter and began to fiddle with her hair.

We passed on the special, ordering filets and lobster tails all around.

After Justin left, Treadwell said, "I imagine you'd like to hear about tomorrow's schedule."

I gulped hard, an involuntary reaction. "How'd you know?"

"The game starts at eleven-fifteen am. You and your party will watch from the Green Room. The Green Room is actually gray, but that's neither here nor there. It's a very comfortable area, I can assure you, adjacent to the visitor's lockers just off center court. You'll be able to view the proceedings from various angles on any of a half-dozen large-screen high-definition color monitors. Prior to halftime, I will personally take you out to the floor, where you'll have two minutes and forty-five seconds to warm up while the studio announcers recap the first half."

"That's a relief," I said. "I wasn't sure if I'd get any practice time."

"We want you to have every advantage. At that point,

we'll escort your party to reserved courtside seats, all the better to obtain dramatic reaction shots."

"Awesome," Amy said.

"When we come back from commercial break, you'll be introduced by Michael Buffer ..."

"*The* Michael Buffer?" I asked. "The fight announcer?"

Angela jumped in excitedly. "The guy who says 'Let's get ready to rumble?'"

Treadwell looked pleased. "The one and only. I told you we do things right at Bigg Fizz. In any event, as soon as he's done with the intros, it's your turn to shine. One shot, one million dollars. Do you have any questions?"

"No, I think you've answered them all."

"Our driver will pick you up tomorrow morning at ten in front of your hotel."

"Same driver?" Angela asked.

"I believe so," Treadwell said. "He's been assigned to you all weekend. Why do you ask?"

"No reason," she said. "He just really knows how to handle a car."

After dinner, we said our goodbyes to Trip Treadwell and headed back to our room. The flashing telephone light indicated another message. It was from Jason, now safely ensconced in his parents' condo. Quickly, I punched in his number. He answered on the third ring.

"Hello?"

"Jason, it's Nick. What took you so long? We were starting to worry."

"Just your typical bad day. About a half-hour after I got my little speeding ticket, I had a blowout."

"Are you okay?"

"Yeah, it gave me a chance to practice my emergency driving maneuvers. But then I was stuck in the middle of nowhere, no cell service, and now where was that asshole cop when I need him? I had to hitch a ride on the back of some old pickup to the nearest town, which

wasn't exactly close. It cost me a hundred bucks for the
tow and two hundred for the tire. They've got you by
the short hairs out there and they know it. When you
make your shot tomorrow, I think I'll buy that gas station just so I can shut it down."

"Another wise investment."

"Anyway, what's the plan?"

I filled him in and told him to meet us in front of the
hotel at ten in the morning.

"See you then," he said pleasantly. "Get a good night's
sleep."

Not likely. For a while, after everybody went to bed,
I listlessly cycled through the TV channels, stopping for
a time on the news or a local talk show or some nature
program. But tonight, even crocodiles versus boa con-
strictors in the South American rainforest couldn't hold
my attention. I was too hot, I was too cold, I couldn't
find a comfortable place for myself, my back itched in a
spot frustratingly out of reach. Briefly, I opened a musty
old paperback that somebody had left behind, a spy
thriller called *The Excelsior File*, but only managed to read
the same sentence over and over. At last, I pulled on my
shoes in disgust.

"Where're you going?" Pam asked sleepily.

"I'm restless," I said. "Thought I'd go for a walk."

"Want company?"

"No. Thanks. I just want to clear my head."

"Okay, don't forget your key."

I padded through the living area, careful not to wake
Amy, and silently closed the door behind me. Out on the
street, the night air had just a whisper of coolness. Jam-
ming my hands into my jeans pockets, I gulped down a
few lungfuls of oxygen and headed toward America West
Arena.

The lights were on, but nobody was home. At night,
the giant saucer-shaped building looks like something
out of *Close Encounters*. At any moment, a door would

open, a ramp would appear, and hundreds of childlike alien creatures would ask for a Bigg Fizz. A whole new untapped market. Maybe it would taste better to them.

Just for fun, I tried a few doors. All locked. Oh well, I'd be inside soon enough. When a fat man in a rent-a-cop uniform started in my direction, I decided to call it a night.

Back at the hotel, I actually forced myself into a few hours of fitful sleep. In my dreams, the little man kept making his shot. Then, sometime before dawn, he missed.

32

I awoke with a start. The luminous green numbers on the digital clock read 5:43. For a moment or two, I didn't have the slightest idea where I was or what I was doing there. Then, as I tried to focus on the unfamiliar furnishings in the gray pre-dawn light, it all came rushing back at once, delivering a well-placed blow to my solar plexus. This was it. The beginning of my big day.

T-minus six hours and counting. Six long agonizing hours. And no help from Mission Control. They were still sound asleep.

I dragged myself out of bed, realizing that it had indeed been a tough week. I didn't feel like crap, exactly. Crap would have been an improvement. My body ached and my head throbbed with what the commercials call "flu-like symptoms." A bad case of pre-game jitters, to be sure. Taking matters into my own hands, I raided the wet bar, blending up a concoction of Bloody Mary mix and Bigg Fizz, using the whole mess to down three Extra-Strength Excedrins. The resulting belch reverberated throughout the room, letting me know I just might survive.

"Good one," Pam said from somewhere behind me.

"You startled me," I said.

"Same here."

"I didn't sleep so good."

"I figured. You tossed and turned all night. Are you okay?"

"I'll let you know."

"You'll feel better after you get some breakfast in you."

We ordered room service. Scrambled eggs, bacon extra crisp, sourdough toast, black coffee. I picked at my food with little enthusiasm, forcing myself to eat as much as I could keep down. Coffee was the key. I needed enough to pull me out of my funk, but not so much as to push me over the edge into caffeine delirium. It was a delicate balancing act, but I pulled it off. By the time I was done with breakfast, I was ready to go. To the bathroom. Which, as any veteran traveler knows, is the most important part of the day. Because, if you leave your room before the urge strikes, you can forget about finding a clean facility. Or even one that flushes.

A half-hour later, emerging into the living room refreshed and five pounds lighter, I was greeted by Amy and Angela, now enjoying room-service breakfasts of their own.

"Jeez, Dad, close the door. You're killing us," Amy said.

"Give me a break. Like you've never fouled the environment."

"I don't even go," she said.

Angela interrupted, "Don't you people have any manners? I'm trying to eat here."

"You're lucky I didn't get into size, shape, color, and consistency."

Angela fixed me with her patented glare, a clear warning to knock it off.

"I need to talk to you," I told her, sitting down. "I had a bad dream last night."

"Who do I look like, Sigmund Freud?"

"Listen. It's about the little man in my head. He missed."

Angela took the news in stride. It wasn't the reaction I was expecting. "Of course he did," she said, nibbling on a piece of bacon.

"What do you mean?" Now I was really confused.

"He's tired, he's bored. It means you're ready. You're peaking at just the right time."

"No shit?"

"No shit. Now leave me alone and let me finish my meal. I'm not a morning person, or haven't you noticed?"

After breakfast, we took turns showering and getting ready to leave. Usually, I have to play the part of drill sergeant, rousing the troops to action. But this morning was different. Everybody knew the importance of being on time.

I showered last. There was still plenty of hot water, one of the many benefits of hotel life. Rick Majerus, former basketball coach of the Utah Utes, lives in a hotel full-time. Makes sense to me. I could get used to that little mint on my pillow.

Still in my towel, I found Amy standing in front of the bed, scratching her head, looking puzzled. There, spread out before her, was my entire collection of gym wear. She took a shirt, matched it with a pair of shorts, stood back and stared for a moment, shook her head, tried a different combination. Finally, she settled on a red-shirt-and-black-shorts ensemble. Plus, the sunglasses.

"That's it," she said. "It's speaking to me."

"What's it saying?"

"It says, 'Here's a man with an intelligent daughter.'"

Pam joined the conversation. "You're only missing one thing."

"What's that?"

She reached into a plastic bag, producing a black baseball cap. On the front, embroidered in silver lettering, was the word "Money."

"It's perfect," I said, simultaneously trying it on and giving her a kiss. "I'm relieved."

"Relieved? About what?"

"That it doesn't say 'Asshole.'"

33

Miraculously, we were downstairs at the curb by 9:57. A minute later, Jason strolled past with an air of exaggerated nonchalance. Doing one of those old movie-comedy double takes, he said, "Well, if it isn't the Nichols family. Imagine running into you here, of all places." He tipped his cap.

"Sorry," I said. "You must have us confused with somebody else. We're the Cleavers."

"Just as well," he said. "Never did like those Nichols people anyway. Too snooty for my tastes."

Pam put an end to our foolishness. "Jason, I swear you've been hanging around Nick too long. You're as nutty as he is."

"She's just jealous," I said. "Need a lift?"

At that very moment, our limo glided to a stop directly in front of us, looking even sleeker and shinier than I remembered. In a heartbeat, Clyde was helping us into the back. It seemed to me that Angela lingered next to Clyde slightly longer than necessary. Pam, her co-conspirator, casually glanced at his left hand.

"No ring," she whispered.

With his usual air of corporate solemnity, Clyde proceeded to drive us across the street to America West Arena. Instead of hassling with the crush of vehicles already jockeying for position in the main parking area, he maneuvered us into a side lot past a "Restricted Access" sign. Flashing some sort of badge at the guard, he shot through the gate and into a reserved parking space directly in front of the "Employees Only" entrance.

"Last stop," Clyde announced, cracking a smile for the first time. Maybe he was loosening up.

"Thank God," Jason said. "My legs were starting to cramp."

As we piled out, I said to Clyde, "Are you joining us?" Angela looked like she was about to faint.

Clyde said, "No, thank you. I'll be waiting right here, listening to the radio."

"Nonsense," I said. "You're like one of the family by now. Come with us. We must have some juice around here."

Hesitantly, Clyde fell in behind us as we made our way toward the entrance. Waiting for us was Trip Treadwell, resplendent in an expensive European business suit.

"Good morning, all!" he said, checking his oyster-shell Rolex. "Right on time."

"Thanks to Clyde here," I touched his shoulder.

"Yes, he's the best," Treadwell agreed.

I took him aside, saying, "What are the chances of Clyde joining the party? He's a great guy."

For the first time since our initial meeting, Treadwell appeared slightly flustered. "Well, er, um," he stammered, "it is somewhat irregular, but under the circumstances, I don't see why not."

"You're in," I told Clyde, giving him a thumb's-up sign. I thought Angela might kiss me.

"Okay, everybody, hold out your hands," Treadwell said. With practiced dexterity, he slapped a plastic hospital-style bracelet around each of our wrists, gold for me, red for everyone else.

"And who's this young man?" he asked when he got to Jason.

"That's Jason McBride, my future son-in-law," I lied, shooting Amy my best shut-your-trap look. "He was unexpectedly detained yesterday. An important legal matter."

"You're an attorney?" Treadwell inquired. Before Jason could respond, he prattled on, "Outstanding profession. The backbone of this great nation. You are to be commended."

"Thank you," Jason said, looking down at his shoes. I'm sure it was to keep from cracking up at this farce.

Treadwell didn't seem to notice. He said, "Well, follow me. Let's get you situated."

He led us through a labyrinth of behind-the-scenes hallways with exposed ductwork and pipes, past boxes stacked high on palettes and industrial-sized dumpsters overflowing with debris. The unmistakable aroma of hot dogs and popcorn wafted along the corridors. From somewhere in the distance, I could hear the faint sounds of organ music and the indecipherable rumblings of the P.A. announcer. Suddenly, my heart skipped and my stomach lurched. This was actually happening, and sooner rather than later. Or, as Amy used to say when she was a little girl, "For reals."

After what felt like the Bataan Death March, our journey ended at the Green Room, which, as Treadwell had informed us, was a sickly gray. I was sure it matched my own complexion.

"Here we are, your new headquarters. Get comfortable, relax, help yourselves to the buffet. I'll be back in about fifteen minutes to see how you're doing."

We thanked him and Treadwell disappeared.

The buffet had a nice selection of fresh fruit and veggies, finger sandwiches, chicken wings, jumbo shrimp, and those little burrito wraps that are all the rage. Not to mention the ubiquitous bottles of Bigg Fizz.

"I'd kill for a Coke," Jason said as he and Clyde swarmed over the food table.

"Not too loud," I warned. "We don't want them to throw us out."

Ordinarily, I'd be right there with them, piling on the goodies. Now, I just wanted to sit back and try to get my head screwed on straight. My emotions were a churning cauldron of fear and excitement, first one, then the other, then both at the same time. Just as I'd begin to get a grip, something—a noise, an extraneous thought, an image on the TV monitors—would shake me up and start the whole cycle again. Each second seemed agonizingly slow, dripping by like the clock hands in a Dali painting. Clearly, I could not survive the next two hours in this condition. Something would have to give.

Something did. Right on schedule, Trip Treadwell breezed into the room, a stack of bright orange clothing in his arms.

"Time to change into your official Bigg Fizz gear," he said cheerily.

We all stopped and stared at him.

"My what?" I asked.

"Bigg Fizz gear. Look, here's a nice T-shirt with matching shorts and an adjustable cap. I love these, don't you? The logo shows up really well on television." The Bigg Fizz logo he spoke of looked as though the letters were made of bubbles. The company probably paid a quarter of a million bucks for it. Six or eight graphics guys at my old firm, including a few interns, could have done a better job.

"Do I really have to wear this stuff?"

"I'm sure they're your size."

"It's not that. My daughter went to a lot of trouble to buy me these special gym clothes, and it would mean a great deal to her if I could wear them."

"That's right," Amy agreed.

"And," I added, "this custom cap was given to me by my father on his deathbed." I held it up proudly.

"Yes, I see," said Treadwell, his eyes narrowing. "Very nice. Very nice indeed. But I'm afraid I'm going to have to pull rank on you this time. Part of the deal is that you promote our product exclusively. It's in your contract. I can show it to you if you'd like."

"That won't be necessary."

"Well, then, I'll leave you to change. If you need anything, just dial zero on the courtesy phone by the sofa."

"Thanks," I said. "You've done enough already."

When Treadwell had gone, Amy came over and patted my hand.

"It's okay, Dad. It doesn't matter."

"Thanks, kid. It matters to me."

"Can you believe that guy? What a freak."

"He's just following the rules. That's why big companies hire people like him."

"I hope he gets fired."

"Nah, he'll probably wind up running the whole show." I reached in my pocket and gave her a handful of singles. "Do your old Dad a favor, will you? See if you can find us some real soft drinks."

The only good thing about the gym-clothes episode was that it pulled me out of my emotional tailspin. Coming out of the bathroom after changing, I asked the assembled multitude, "Is this the real me or what?"

Pam looked like she just bit into a lemon. "Positively hideous."

"Nobody should have to wear that," Angela weighed in. "Unless your name is Sunkist."

I asked Clyde, "What do you think?"

"Well, technically, I'm still on the Bigg Fizz payroll, so I have to choose my words carefully."

"And?"

"Fuckin' ugly."

The resulting laughter was just the tonic I needed.

Amy returned with Cokes for everyone. It was now 11:14. One minute before tip-off. An hour, give or take, until halftime. I staked out a position on the love seat. The rest of our group arranged themselves on the oversized couch. Somehow, Angela and Clyde wound up next to each other. On the audio feed, Jim Nantz and Billy Packer, the CBS announcing team, were making last-minute preparations, while the network aired a Miller Genuine Draft spot. Nantz was tapping on his earpiece, saying, "There's some ungodly static on this thing. Can somebody get me another please? Hurry!" Under normal circumstances, this kind of glimpse into the inner circle of sports broadcasting would have fascinated me. But these were anything but normal circumstances.

The game started as soon as the MGD ad was over. UCLA took control of the tip-off and promptly lost the ball out of bounds. It was the last play I remember seeing. Closing my eyes, concentrating on my breathing, trying to draw air all the way down to my diaphragm, I entered some sort of trance state where time lost all meaning. Either that, or I fell asleep. Because the next thing I knew, I opened my eyes to find a CBS camera less than a foot from my face. On the audio, Packer said, "Now there's a man with ice water in his veins. You'd think he did this every day." I looked up to see my very own astonished mug on network television, before they cut away to an Arizona team meeting on the sidelines. At that very instant, Trip Treadwell entered the room, announcing "Five minutes to halftime."

Alarmed to say the least, I asked no one in particular, "Was anybody going to wake me?"

"It was my call," Angela said. "I thought it was better to let you zone out."

"That's true," Pam said. "We didn't know what to do."

"How you feelin'?" Angela asked.

Shaking myself, I said, "A little stiff."

I spent the next four minutes doing stretching exercises.

With one minute to go, Treadwell said, "It's time."

I walked over to the most important people in my life.

"I love you," Pam said. "No matter what."

"Same here," I said, giving her a hug that I never wanted to end. "More than ever."

Amy said, "Just remember, Pop, you still look cool." She gave me a kiss on the cheek.

"Thanks, kiddo."

"Good luck, Nick," Jason said. "Hurl the ringer." I had to laugh. It was a line from my favorite movie, *One Flew Over the Cuckoo's Nest*. We shook hands.

"Go get 'em," Clyde said. "By the way, I've just canceled my no-tip policy."

"Not a problem," I said. I turned to face Angela, standing there with her hands on her hips. "Hey, Coach, any last-second advice?"

She just shook her head. "You know what to do." It was the best advice I've ever heard.

"It's time," Trip Treadwell repeated, a bit ominously, I thought. With a glance back and a little wave, I followed him out of the room and through a long tunnel.

34

It was the closest thing I've had to an out-of-body experience. Moving through the dark tunnel into the light. But no trip to the hereafter, as far as I know, ever included cheerleaders, marching bands, and 20,000 screaming fans. They were like loud colorful amoebas, part of some larger creature that throbbed and pulsated and flowed into every corner of the arena. When I emerged onto the hardwood floor, the brightness was disorienting. No amount of mental imagery could have prepared me for the size and scope of my surroundings. Suddenly, I felt very small and insignificant, the way you do when you watch an interview with Nelson Mandela. The flood of sensations overwhelmed my ability to assimilate them. As I followed Treadwell to the top of the key, I felt my mind fragment and detach, so that part of me was watching the proceedings from a safe distance.

Treadwell handed me a basketball. *The* basketball. I reached for it automatically, as he said, "You can warm up until your introduction. Then you're good to go. Any questions?"

Questions? I couldn't remember my own name. After an awkward silence, Treadwell said, "Well, good luck, then." He held out his hand and I shook it. It must have felt like a dead fish to him. He turned and disappeared into the crowd.

The basketball was comfortingly familiar, a twin to the one I'd been practicing with, possibly born in the same

Wilson factory, then separated at birth. I bounced it a few times, positioned myself at the appropriate spot and let it go. It hit the back iron and bounced straight up in the air before coming down through the hoop. "Maybe I should save that for later," I remember thinking. The rim was a little tighter than the one at the rec center, but nothing I couldn't handle. A teenage boy under the backboard retrieved the ball, passing it crisply back to me. I took it and launched another shot. It was short by a few inches, but I was beginning to loosen up, getting a feel for my surroundings.

My next four or five attempts were all good. Later, when I watched the videotape, I heard Jim Nantz comment, "Well, Billy, Alan Nichols looks pretty good out there. I understand he's from Las Vegas. What do you think the odds are at the sports books?"

Packer replied, "I don't know, Jim, but I'm sure a few NBA teams could use his services." Both men chuckled.

I lost track of how many more shots I took, but most of them went in. Then, all at once, the lights dimmed and a familiar voice boomed, "Ladies and gentlemen, may I have your attention please." I turned to see a tuxedoed figure at the opposite end of the court. The crowd, recognizing Michael Buffer, burst into spontaneous applause before giving him what passed for rapt attention. Buffer, the man who made a fortune on the strength of one memorable catch phrase, was quite possibly the luckiest man in America.

"Ladies and gentlemen," he repeated. "The NCAA, in cooperation with Bigg Fizz, the soft drink with twice the carbonation of the leading brand, is proud to present the Million Dollar Challenge. And now, from Las Vegas, Nevada, in the bright orange trunks, let's have a warm America West Arena welcome for Alan Nichols!" Scattered clapping and cheers. "Mr. Nichols will take one shot from three-point range for one million dollars! Are you ready?" The crowd screamed "Yes!" I think I tried, too, but the words died in my throat. "I can't hear you," Buffer said. Maybe he was going deaf. The crowd screamed again, even louder. "Then … let's get READDDYYY TO RUUUMMMBBBLE!" The place went absolutely apeshit. Go figure.

My turn. Everything I'd done, thought, learned, imagined during the last four weeks, coming into crystalline focus at this precise moment. Now. My conscious mind had already clicked off and I found myself on extreme autopilot. Standing at the three-point line, bouncing the ball, once, twice, going through my little routine, the way I'd done thousands of times before, letting my body take over, I felt everything disappear. First, the crowd, then the noise and commotion, until it was just the ball, the basket, and me, all bathed in an eerie silence. I looked up to see that the basket was roughly the size of a Hula-Hoop. A strange calm enveloped me, a certainty that came from deep within. For the first time in my adult life, I said a prayer, just a simple "Thank you," a page from Angela's playbook. Not to kiss God's ass, but to express my gratitude for all that had happened. By way of an "Amen," I fired the ball toward the basket.

It felt as good as any shot I've ever taken. Flying perfectly off my index finger, directly at the hoop, just the right amount of backspin, the ball traveling a pre-programmed trajectory, so much like a guided missile I could almost see the flames shooting out the back, leaving a vapor trail all the way to the target. Instead of a "bang," it arrived with a soft "swish," so gentle the net barely moved. For a second, neither did I. I simply stood there, taking it all in, uncomprehending, waiting for my mind to catch up to what my body had just accomplished.

And then, bedlam. The roar of the crowd rolling in like the ocean, a swirling, pounding, crashing tsunami of sound. Suddenly surrounded by my loved ones, Pam and Amy throwing their arms around me, shouting, "I knew you could do it!" and "Way to go" and "I love you!"

Angela hanging back, looking so pleased, I could've sworn she'd nailed the shot herself. Jason, smiling like he just hung ten on a wicked twenty-footer at Waimea, pumping his fist and shouting, "We're going to Disney World!" Trip Treadwell, still the picture of corporate cool, waiting for his opportunity to retake center stage. Cameramen and NCAA officials and Bigg Fizz reps, all crowding and pushing and jostling for position. Bonnie Bernstein, the CBS courtside reporter, a head shorter than anybody else on the floor, working her way through the throng, shoving a microphone in my face, asking, "When did you know it was good?" And, before I could answer, cupping her hand over her headphones and saying to a disembodied voice back in the booth, "What do you mean? Say that again? I didn't quite hear you. Are you sure?" And me, not knowing what was going on, suddenly getting a funny feeling in the pit of my stomach, like when the phone rings in the middle of the night. And Bernstein saying, this time to the camera, "I've just been informed of a developing situation. Somebody high up in the Bigg Fizz organization is reviewing the tape, claiming the shot is invalid, that Alan Nichols stepped on the line." She turned to face me. "If that is indeed the case, what's your comment?" Her eyes bore through me. The crowd stopped as if somebody hit the pause button. The building was again silent. And I heard myself saying, completely off guard, "Uh, I don't know." And Bernstein, looking at the camera, said, "We'll be back after a commercial break to try to sort this all out."

35

The commercial break lasted four minutes. During that brief time span, a hundred things happened at once. While Bonnie Bernstein continued communicating with the booth, Trip Treadwell took me by the arm and led me to the sidelines. The mob on the floor followed en masse, as if pulled by some magnetic force. Word must have gotten around the arena in a hurry, because 20,000 voices took up the chant, "Bullshit! Bullshit! Bullshit!" I remember wondering how that would play on network television. You couldn't bleep an entire building, could you?

Treadwell was on his cell phone, saying, "Yes, I understand, but ... no, I realize it's in the agreement, of course, but ... have you considered the public-relations implications ... I'm not arguing with you ... no, I don't want to look for another job ..." He snapped the phone shut, looking pale beneath his tan.

"That was Mr. Stanley. He's reviewed the videotape twice, and he's holding firm. 'The rules are the rules.' That's a direct quote. Mr. Stanley has always been a stickler where the rules are concerned."

Now I was regaining my senses, because I could feel myself getting pissed. "What kind of chickenshit operation are you running here?" I demanded. "I made the goddamned shot. Everybody in America saw it."

"That's right," Jason seconded. He and Pam and Amy and Angela and Clyde had Treadwell surrounded. He must have felt a little like Custer. Pam squeezed my hand in support.

Treadwell held his ground. "Mr. Stanley is the final arbiter on this matter."

"So where does that leave us?" I asked.

"Fifty thousand dollars to the good."

"Big deal," Angela said. "I'll bet you planned this all along."

"I can assure you that's not the case," Treadwell replied.

"Oh yeah? How?" Pam wanted to know.

I asked, "What if I refuse the money?"

"Mr. Stanley says you have two choices. Take it or leave it."

"I want to talk to this shit-for-brains," I said. "Tell him to get his fat ass down here."

"Mr. Stanley is quite fit, actually, for a man his age. And he doesn't talk to anybody."

"He'll talk to me. Doesn't he realize how bad this looks? It's gonna be a PR nightmare."

"Mr. Stanley is a man of deep convictions. He won't budge."

Amy looked like she was about to cry. "Dad, he can't do this to you. *Do* something!"

"Honey, I'm trying."

"Bigg Fizz blows!" she blurted out.

"There's your new slogan, Treadwell," I said.

Bonnie Bernstein entered the fray. "We have your shot cued up on the monitor at the scorer's table," she said. "Would you like to take a look?"

"Damn right I would."

We followed her the dozen or so feet to where the monitor sat. On the screen, my image stood frozen, like a life-sized ice sculpture. She barked, "Roll tape!" and my video counterpart sprang into action, bouncing the ball twice before drilling the three-pointer. It looked as perfect as I'd imagined. "Back it up," Bernstein instructed.

"Run frame by frame. Okay, isolate and freeze." The camera zoomed in on my lower extremities. Even up close in super slow motion, it was hard to tell. My foot may or may not have brushed the line. It was by no means clearcut. The crowd increased the rhythm and intensity of their "Bullshit" chant, and I realized they were watching along with us on the giant Jumbotron screen hanging from the arena rafters.

"Hear that?" I asked rhetorically. "They've got a point."

"Let's check it from another angle," Bernstein said. Again, the result was ambiguous. I turned to face Treadwell.

"This is what your boss is watching?"

"Yes."

"What do *you* think?"

"What I think is irrelevant."

"I hope you're proud of yourself," I said. Turning to Bernstein, I asked, "What's *your* opinion? You've got a lot more experience than we have."

"Too close to call. But if you pressed me on it, I'd say you made your shot."

"Thank you."

"How old is this Stanley, anyway?" Pam asked.

Treadwell thought for a moment. "Mid-sixties, I'd say."

"Does he wear glasses?"

"No."

"Maybe he should."

Bernstein interrupted. "I hate to do this to you folks, but we're back from break in ninety seconds. We need to wrap up."

"Okay, gang," I said to my group. "Now what?"

"I'll sue the bastards," Jason pounded a fist into a palm, still into his lawyer role.

"Maybe, but it could take years, they'll eat us alive, and we could still wind up losing."

Pam said, "I don't care. This is just wrong. We can't let them get away with it."

"She's right, Dad," Amy said. "This is messed up."

I said to Angela, "You're awfully quiet. What are you thinking?"

"What I'm thinking is, if this was the playground, we'd just go double or nothing. Too bad we can't do that now."

Jason stopped cold. "Why the hell not? What do we have to lose?"

"Everything," I said. "What if I miss?"

"Then you'll go down swinging."

"What about your hot dog stand?"

"No worries."

I shook my head. "The old man'll never go for it."

"Can't hurt to ask," from Pam.

"Sixty seconds," from Bernstein.

"Does she have to keep saying that?" from Amy.

I took a long slow breath. "Is it unanimous?"

"Damn straight," from Jason.

"I was lookin' for a job when I got this one," from Angela.

"I'm in," from Amy.

"Fuckin' A," from Pam. I did a double take. In all the years we've been together, I've never heard Pam use the "F" word. Not counting eight hours in labor.

I looked her square in the eyes and asked, "Are you sure?"

She matched my gaze and nodded.

"Fuckin' A!" I repeated. Our new mantra. We all clasped hands like a team breaking huddle. "Treadwell!" I yelled. "Get your boss on the horn. I've got a proposal for him."

36

And that's how I found myself back at the three-point line. Harrison Stanley the Third, as it turned out, was a betting man. The proposition intrigued him, plain and simple.

CBS knew a good story when they saw one. The boys in the booth juggled the halftime festivities to make room for my second shot.

Weeks later, when I finally got around to watching the tape, I heard Jim Nantz say, "Here we go again, Billy. Can you believe it?"

"I like this Nichols fella," Packer replied. "He's got *cojones* the size of melons."

A few seconds of silence passed before Nantz said, "You *do* have a way with words."

As for me, there was a subtle shift in my internal landscape. It was like ramping up for a critical board meeting, only to find out, at the last minute, that it had been postponed, then rescheduled for later that day. I was still confident, but without the overpowering sense of certainty. The game face was there, but not the focus. Whereas I had been numb the first go-around, now my nerves were slightly worn at the edges. Looking back, I think it's because I had something extra to prove. I wanted it even more this time. Not only for the money, but to justify the trust and faith of my own personal rooting section. And to deliver a big "fuck you" to Mr. Harrison Stanley the Third and his flunkies at Bigg Fizz.

Time being of the essence, there was none of the carnival atmosphere of the first attempt. It was all muscle memory. Imagining myself back in the East Las Vegas Recreation Center, I stepped up to the line, wiped my hands on my shorts, took a couple of deep breaths to clear my head, went through my usual pre-shot ritual (paying particular attention to my feet), and sent the ball on its way.

My shot was just as straight and true as the first one. Better, even. As it fell halfway through the hoop, I allowed myself the luxury of a small satisfied smirk. I was already counting the money when something—call it fate, karma, hubris, or just a nasty patch of bad air—flicked it ever so gently out of the basket. I've seen this in games from time to time, and I still don't understand why it happens. Maybe I shouldn't have ditched that particular physics class. Nevertheless, the ball hovered on the rim for a moment, not sure which way to drop. At last, it chose the path of least resistance, landing with a thud on the hardwood floor. Instantly, 20,000 cheers turned into a single disappointed groan, finally falling away into an uneasy silence.

The energy drained out of me as if somebody had pulled the plug. I stood there in disbelief, shoulders slumping, knees buckling, mouth hanging open like a fish gasping for air. I didn't know whether to sit down, throw up, or pass out. Whoever said "Losing hurts worse than winning feels good" sure knew what he was talking about. A million thoughts battered their way into my head, all of them foul. You're a loser, they said. You let everyone down. You blew it. You gripped. You belong in the Choke Artist's Hall of Fame, right next to Scott Norwood, Mitch Williams, and Greg Norman. The bad guys win again. No money, no consolation prize, no nothing. Go home, they said. You make us sick.

Losers don't get mobbed by adoring fans. Only my family and friends were there to help me off the court.

"I'm so sorry," I kept saying.

"It's okay," they said. "It's okay."

A bouquet of microphones materialized in front of me. "How do you feel?" reporters shouted. Do they learn that in journalism school, or does it just come naturally? Either way, I was in no mood.

"How do I feel?" I repeated. "Like hammered crap."

As I left the floor, I thought I heard one of them say something about a "valiant effort." Funny, it didn't seem valiant to me. Just dumb.

37

We checked out of the Presidential Suite later that day. Technically, we were entitled to stay overnight, but I couldn't get out of there fast enough. I'd had enough of Bigg Fizz's hospitality. We threw our clothes and other belongings haphazardly into our bags, wrinkles be damned. Nobody said a word. Like the Prisoner in the classic British TV series, I was enmeshed in a giant bubble of gloom. Instinctively, the women knew to just let me be.

Trip Treadwell hadn't been that perceptive. Earlier, he'd followed us out of the arena, saying "Slow down a minute, I'm very sorry about all this, I feel terrible, I really do, but it was out of my hands, I was just …"

I stopped and turned to face him. "I know, I know. You were just following orders."

"That's right," he said, pleased that I seemed to understand his position. "Following orders," he repeated.

"Yeah. You and Eichmann."

"Who?"

"Just some guy I used to work with at the agency."

He put out his hand. "No hard feelings, then?"

"No," I said, shaking his hand in a perfunctory manner. "No feelings of any kind."

We rented a car for the trip home, a big-ass Cadillac. (Pam had an upgrade coupon in her purse.) After our experience on the plane, nobody was looking forward to a return to the not-so-friendly skies. I thought a nice long drive, cruising down the highway in our metal and glass cocoon, would give me some time to think. Lord knows I had plenty to think about. Like how to earn a living, for starters.

Angela and Jason accompanied us to the car-rental place, where we said our goodbyes. Jason, of course, was zooming back to Vegas in his BMW.

"Pay attention to that radar detector," I instructed. "Like I tell Amy, they don't let you keep getting tickets indefinitely."

"Yes, Dad."

For the hundredth time, I tried to apologize for missing the shot, but he cut me off.

"Forget it," he said. "I knew the risks. If I had to do it again, I wouldn't change a thing."

"That means a lot to me."

"Besides," he said with a crooked grin. "I'm gonna go make hot dogs." He kissed the girls and headed for the exit.

I turned my attention to Angela. "Well, Coach, I wish I'd won you some money."

"It's all good."

"How can you say that?"

"In the first place, I haven't exactly been working for free these last four weeks. And you know what else? You reminded me how good it feels to be on a basketball court. That's how it was back in the day."

"Happy to be of service."

"We sure punked those young pups, didn't we?

My face lit up at the memory. "You can say that again! Listen, are you sure you won't drive home with us?"

"Nah, I'm gonna stay on for a couple days," she said slyly.

"Suit yourself. Call us when you get back."

"I got your number."

"You sure do."

"You gonna be okay?" she asked.

"Yeah, I'm always okay."

Abruptly, she gave me a strong, rather awkward hug. She was so solid, it was like embracing a statue.

"Never forget, you made your shot," she said. "You're still Money."

"Thanks, Coach. Thanks for everything."

"No, thank you."

Watching her leave the rental agency, I was grateful she didn't look back. I didn't want her to see me wiping my eyes.

"Okay," I said, wrapping an arm around my two favorite women, "let's blow this Popsicle stand."

38

The drive home got off to a shaky start. After enduring my moping for the first half-hour, Pam glared at me across the expanse of the Caddy's front seat and said, "That's enough."

"Enough what?" I asked, feigning ignorance.

"You know what," she said. "I'm not sitting in this car with you for the next four hours if you're going to act like this."

"How do you expect me to act?"

"Like a functioning member of this family."

"You mean I'm not entitled to drive quietly and lick my wounds?"

"Not on *my* time."

"Yeah, Dad," Amy chimed in from somewhere in the back. "You're no fun at all. Lighten up."

"Sorry. I always get like this when I lose a million dollars. Two million, if you want to get picky about it."

"You've still got your health, and a mind that works, sometimes, and people who love you. So knock it off," Pam ordered.

"At least let us listen to the radio," Amy pleaded.

I flipped the switch and set it on scan. "I doubt if we'll pick up anything out here in the middle of nowhere."

But we did. An oldies station was doing a tribute to Motown and before we knew it, we were singing along to "I Can't Help Myself," and "Where Did Our Love Go?" and "R-E-S-P-E-C-T." I've got to hand it to the girls, it's hard to wallow in self-pity when the music's cranked to eleven and you're playing drums on the dash. After a while, I was feeling a little better, despite myself.

Eventually, though, the signal faded and the scanner locked onto a sports station. Before I could hit the button, the announcer said, "In more hoops action, the Arizona Wildcats got past the pesky UCLA Bruins, seventy-three to seventy, despite a double-double by All-American point guard Jamal Martinez. Arizona sophomore forward Ike Brown sank the winning three-pointer as time expired in regulation. But the real drama took place at halftime ... "

I made a move toward the radio, but Pam grabbed my hand.

"Leave it," she said. "I want to hear this."

The announcer continued, "... when Alan Nichols of Las Vegas, winner of the Bigg Fizz Challenge, appeared to hit the million dollar shot from the top of the key. However, after officials of the Bigg Fizz Company overruled the decision, claiming that Nichols stepped on the line, he talked them into letting him try again, this time double or nothing. Unfortunately, his second shot went in and out. We have not been able to reach Nichols for comment. Meanwhile, our sources tell us that Bigg Fizz has been inundated with calls from irate consumers, and impromptu demonstrations have sprung up at a number of regional bottling plants, as well as at their corporate headquarters in Riverside, California. In other sports news ..."

"Well, I'll be damned," I said. "I never dreamt this was such a big story."

Pam said, "See, people are rallying around you. Maybe Stanley will change his mind."

"Don't hold your breath. He's a stubborn old asshole. I'm glad he's on the hot seat, but you want to know something?"

"What?"

"I don't give a shit what happens."

Pam frowned in disapproval. "Here we go again …"

"I mean it," I protested. "This last month taught me a lot of stuff. Like what's really important."

"Well, that's a shocker. What brought this on?"

"I don't know. It just sort of came to me. Weird, huh?"

Pam slid across the seat and cuddled up next to me. "That's more like it," she said, kissing my neck.

"Oh, puh-leeze!" Amy said. "Are you two gonna get mushy?"

"Maybe," I said. "You want out?"

"No." She leaned back and closed her eyes. "Wake me when we get home."

We drove on for another hour, not needing to talk, Pam with her head on my shoulder. It was strange. I felt better than I had a right to, certainly not like a man who'd just had a fortune snatched from his outstretched hands. But there was no denying it. My fifteen minutes of fame were up, I had no job prospects, but I still had that winning attitude. Angela was right. I made the shot. It didn't matter what anybody else thought. Nobody could take that away from me. A guy who could do that could do anything.

After a while, I spotted a sign that read, "Sedona, 18 Miles."

"Hey," I said to Pam. "How anxious are you to get home?

"Not that anxious," she said. "Why?"

"What do you think about a little side trip to Sedona? I've always wanted to see that place."

"You mean we're actually doing something spontaneous?"

"You don't have to sound so surprised."

"Stunned is more like it."

"Enough already! Do you want to go or not?"

"Sure!"

I turned left at the sign and we traveled along a picturesque, tree-lined highway that eventually dumped us into a spectacular valley surrounded by sheer red cliffs and towering monoliths. It was like nothing I've seen on Earth. Mars, perhaps. Most tourist spots are a letdown when you finally see them in person, but this was better than advertised. I motioned for Pam to wake Amy.

"Are we home yet?" she asked sleepily.

"Slight change in plans," Pam said. "We're taking an unscheduled vacation."

"No way!" Amy said excitedly.

"Way," Pam replied, speaking Amy's native tongue.

"You don't have anything going on tomorrow, do you?" I asked Amy.

"Just school."

"Can you miss a few classes?"

"No problem."

"Then we're on vacation."

We checked into the first decent motel we saw, a Hampton Inn situated on the main drag. Because it was a Sunday afternoon, we had no trouble getting a room. Most of the other guests had already bailed out, leaving early enough to get home in time for the work week ahead. In the lobby, Amy grabbed a handful of colorful brochures from the rack.

"Look," she said. "We can go four-wheeling or horse-back riding or ballooning or ..."

"How about some lunch?" I interrupted. "I think better on a full stomach."

"Where's your sense of adventure?" she demanded.

"Somewhere back in Phoenix."

We found a Mexican restaurant near our hotel. Over a tasty meal of seafood fajitas, we pored over our recreational options, finally deciding on something called a Pink Jeep Tour, which would give us an informative off-road overview of the area. Pam called from the restaurant and made a reservation for the next morning. In the meantime, the girls were going shopping. They said I could tag along if I kept my mouth shut and didn't look at my watch every five minutes.

"I'll try," I said. "But no promises."

We spent the better part of the afternoon wandering through art galleries and shops and boutiques, all of which had the same kind of Southwestern theme. Within a half-hour, I'd had my fill of turquoise jewelry, Navajo rugs, Hopi kachina dolls, and oil paintings by popular local artists. But Pam and Amy were just getting warmed up. Each time we entered a new store, they squealed with delight, as if it wasn't exactly like the one next door. When Pam shelled out two bucks apiece for little desert stones, I knew it was time to leave.

"You're paying for rocks," I pointed out to her.

"They're special rocks," she said. "They have healing powers."

"Yeah, they heal the store's bottom line."

"You're such a cynic."

"I could go into the desert and get better rocks for free."

"Not like these. Look how pretty they are," she said, dropping thirty dollars' worth into a small leather pouch with a $9.95 price tag on it. "Here's one I picked out just for you." She handed me some sort of pink crystal. "Rose quartz. It gives you peace and tranquility."

"It's giving me a headache." After all these years, I know when to give up. Besides, if I couldn't find a job, we could make soup out of it. I took the quartz, gave Pam a quick kiss, and backed out of the shop. "I'm gonna get some fresh air. Why don't I meet you back at the Mexican restaurant in, say, two hours. That should give you enough time, right?"

She looked mildly disappointed. "I suppose."

Safely outside, I strolled past more store fronts, careful not to set foot in any of them. Eventually, at the end of the block, I saw something that captured my interest. An old-fashioned ice-cream parlor. Inside, it reminded me of a place I used to hang out at as a kid. Little white wrought-iron tables, candy-striped chairs, a speckled Formica counter with those red-vinyl revolving stools. Awash in boyhood memories, I bellied up to the bar and ordered a banana split. When it came, it looked like the Matterhorn and was almost as expensive. Too bad nostalgia doesn't apply to prices. Nevertheless, I sat myself down at a window table and, watching the world go by, slowly and deliberately polished off every last mouthful. Everyone knows calories don't count when you're on vacation. Afterward, I waddled over to a park bench under a big gnarled tree and dozed like an old man recovering from his third game of shuffleboard. At least I didn't stick my hand down my pants like my Uncle Nate.

My internal clock nudged me awake at 5:50. Still groggy, I made my way back to the restaurant, where I waited for the shoppers to be late. Sure enough, they showed up at 6:30, moving like pack mules, weighted down with bags and boxes and a large rectangular object, neatly wrapped in brown paper, that could only be one of those desert landscapes I detest. That was the danger of leaving professional consumers with no adult supervision.

"Looks like you did some serious damage," I commented.

"Not so bad," Pam countered. "We found some great sales."

"Yeah, Dad, we saved a ton of money."

"I know how you can save even more money," I said. It's my standard reply, but it never seems to sink in.

They laughed condescendingly and changed the subject.

"What do you want to do about dinner?" Pam asked.

"I'm not very hungry," I said, declining to tell them about my mid-day snack. "Whatever you decide is fine with me."

While Pam thought for a moment, her gaze fell on my shirt. "What's that?"

"What?"

"You have a splotch."

"Where?"

"Right there," she said, indicating a spot about three inches below my collar. "It looks like chocolate."

"I have no idea," I lied. I've always been a lousy liar.

"You had a sundae or something, didn't you?"

"What if I did? There's no law against it."

"Now *we* have to get one."

"Fine."

They threw their junk in the car and followed me to the ice-cream parlor, where Pam had a hot- fudge sundae and Amy devoured a triple scoop of Oreo cookie dough. Being a model of self-discipline, I settled for a root beer float. Somebody has to set an example.

When we were done, we talked Amy out of going to a movie and returned to our room instead. It had been a very long day. Kicking off my shoes, I collapsed into bed like a man under anesthesia. "Count backwards from one hundred," the doctor always says. It's a trick. I was asleep before reaching ninety-eight.

39

"Hold on tight," said Chuck, our Pink Jeep Tour guide. "We're driving up to the top of that ridge." The ridge he spoke of appeared, to my untrained eye, to be at a ninety-degree angle. Hundreds of sharp craggy rocks littered what could only charitably be called our path. Huddled together in the back seat, Pam crushed my hand and Amy screamed, "Go for it!" Unless the jeep had a jet engine I wasn't aware of, I harbored a few doubts about its ability to successfully negotiate the climb. After all, the only jeep I'd ever been in was a Grand Cherokee, and it had enough problems just making it to the store. Of course, underneath the shocking pink paint job, this was a real jeep, and it made the climb with relative ease, the squealing of tires and grinding of gears notwithstanding. After being tossed around the back seat like three crash-test dummies, we found ourselves at the top of a barren granite mesa with a bird's eye view of the entire valley.

Chuck smiled and said, "If you think that was fun, wait'll we go back down." He was a tall sinewy man in his mid-fifties, with a bushy gray mustache and dark eyes that crinkled at the corners. He seemed like a guy who enjoyed his work.

"Have you ever gotten stuck up here?" I asked.

"I haven't, but some of the other fellas have. A month or so ago, one of our jeeps dropped its tranny on a rock not too far from here."

"What happened then?"

"The driver sat back, ate his lunch, and waited for the cavalry. Our company has more than fifty of these babies."

I whistled. "That's a lot of pink paint."

"You folks want to get out and stretch your legs, maybe take a few pictures?"

"Sure." We'd bought one of those throwaway cameras at the company's gift shop. While we took turns clicking away, I asked Chuck, "So how long you been doing this?"

"Oh, about two years."

"What'd you do before?"

"Investment banker in the Bay Area."

"No kidding. How'd you wind up here?"

"My wife and I were on vacation and fell in love with the place. I called my boss, my broker, and my real-estate agent, and told them to cash us out."

"Just like that?"

"Yeah, pretty spur of the moment. Best decision I ever made. Except it's starting to get crowded. Too many guys like me, I guess."

"People ruin everything," I agreed.

"It's still a million times better than the city. I mean, where else are you gonna get views like this?"

"The Omnimax Theater?"

He grinned. "You ready to hit the road? There's plenty more to see."

Chuck was right. During the next two hours, he showed us an actual earthquake fault (dormant, he said), cypress trees growing out of solid rock, prehistoric fish fossils (the entire area used to be covered by ocean, according to Chuck), and a massive, red-rock, bell-shaped monolith called a "vortex." Apparently, Sedona is the Vortex Capital of the World. Local Indian legend has it that vortexes (vortices?) are giant earth-energy magnets, known for their spiritual and physical healing properties. Although I didn't feel magically transformed, the absolute peacefulness of the area was beginning to untie the knots in my stomach. I was like a deep-sea diver entering a decompression chamber before returning to the surface. Essentially, it kept my head from exploding.

The tour was over all too soon. I stuffed a twenty into Chuck's tip box, saying we'd be sure to ask for him if we ever came back.

"I'll be here," he said.

We checked out of our motel, picked up some sub sandwiches on the way out of town, and began the drive back to Las Vegas. Soon, Pam and Amy were dozing and I was alone with my thoughts, not always the best place to be. The trip was uneventful. No turbulence, no sudden drop in cabin pressure, no near-death experiences. Just an increasing sense of dread as we got closer and closer to home. Turning the corner onto our street, I somehow expected the house to be gone. Burned to the ground or stolen by a gang of particularly enterprising burglars. But it was still there, right where we left it. Everything appeared to be in order. I was vaguely disappointed.

We were tired, but not weary. Ignoring the mail and the infernal blinking of the answering machine, I fixed myself a bowl of Wheaties, "Dinner of Champions," and headed upstairs. While I ate, Pam clicked through the five hundred or so cable channels. Luckily, none of them featured me. Maybe the furor had already died down. By the second go-around, I was half-asleep. The last thing I remember was Pam gently removing the cereal bowl from my hand.

The next thing I knew, Pam was shaking me and yelling, "Nick, wake up! Wake up!"

"What? What?" I rasped through the sandpaper in my throat. "You're giving me a heart attack."

"You've got to hear this!"

"What time is it?"

"A little past midnight."

"Can't it wait 'til morning?"

"No!"

"Is it bad?"

"Just listen." She activated the playback on the answering machine. The first message was from the producer of "The Today Show." The next was from "Good Morning America." Followed, in rapid succession, by "Regis & Kelly," "Larry King," "David Letterman," "The Tonight Show," "Oprah," "ESPN," "Jim Rome," and "Howard Stern." But it was the last message that really woke me up. "Mr. Nichols, this is Victoria Bradford from the Coca-Cola Company in Atlanta," the voice said. "Please call back at your earliest convenience. We have a proposition we think you'll find most interesting."

EPILOGUE

By now, I've seen it more times than I care to remember. The TV commercial opens with actual footage of me, making my million-dollar shot. Then, quick cuts of the crowd, the chaos, the controversy, and the miss. From what I understand, the images are so well-known, they've become part of the cultural mythology. Like Billy Buck's infamous through-the-legs error, denying the Red Sox yet another shot at the Fall Classic. Each time, I hope for a different ending, but it's always the same. Halfway into the spot, the announcer says in deep serious tones, "Sometimes life isn't fair. Sometimes we can't do anything about it. Sometimes we can." Close-up of me, at corporate headquarters, a big goofy grin plastered all over my mug, accepting one of those oversized promotional checks courtesy of the Coca-Cola Company. A check for two million dollars. Me again, thanking Pam and Angela and Jason and Coke and everybody else who made this all possible. And the announcer, ending with an emotional, "It's just our way of saying 'Good job, Nick.'" Coke theme up and under, cut to logo and slogan. Not a dry eye in the house, including mine. Another example of the awesome power of the media.

Three months later, that commercial is the hardest thing for me to get used to. More than the print ads. More than the billboards. Even more than the money. Flipping through the channels, any time day or night, *bam*, there it is. Usually, I click right by, but every now and then I stop to watch, to relive the strange events of my recent past. It's gotten to where I'm not even sure of my own memories, they've become so intertwined with the images on the screen. That damn campaign shows no sign of petering out, either. In the business, we say it has "legs." It's captured the imagination of a public that loves to root for the underdog. Hey, Coke isn't number one for nothing. They know how to put their foot on the neck of the competition. And crush it with one short brutal stomp.

Speaking of the competition, in the weeks following the Bigg Fizz fiasco, sales plummeted thirty-seven percent and their stock fell even more. A month later, Harrison Stanley the Third was out on his ass, victim of a board of director's coup. He hasn't been heard from since. I'm not overly concerned. According to the news reports, the company eased his pain with a generous golden-parachute package, guaranteeing him a nice cushy landing. Certainly more than he deserves. Oh, and the new CEO? Guy by the name of Walter "Trip" Treadwell. Who was it that said, "Be careful what you wish for?"

The first thing I did after getting the money was send ten percent to Angela and Jason. Two hundred large apiece, leaving us with $1.6 million before taxes. More on that later. Then, despite my protests, Pam and I made the talk-show circuit. Mainly, Pam wanted to see Manhattan, which is where most of the programs originate. The trip is a blur, as far as I'm concerned. Two quick impressions: Katie Couric is better looking in person. Geraldo isn't.

After returning to Las Vegas, I paid off my bet by guest-hosting the "Biff and Barf Show." I must have been okay, because when I was done, the program director offered me a job. I respectfully declined. The last thing I want is to be responsible for putting those two back on the street.

A week or so later, when the calls began to taper off,

Pam, Amy and I sat down with a big Rand McNally Atlas and made plans to get out of town permanently. Our list of rules and restrictions quickly eliminated most of the country. "No snow." That wiped out the entire East Coast. "No humidity." Goodbye South and Midwest. "No hurricanes, mosquitoes, alligators." See ya later, Florida. "No floods or tornados." Put a big X through Texas, Kansas, Oklahoma. "No deserts." Forget about Arizona, Utah, and of course, Nevada. And, for good measure, no cities with more than 250,000 people. That's how we wound up here.

After Amy's spring semester at UNLV, we bought a twenty-eight-foot Bounder RV and headed for the west coast. A few weeks later, we somehow managed to narrow our choices to three communities: San Luis Obispo, California; Olympia, Washington; and Eugene, Oregon. Amy made the final decision. She fell in love with the University of Oregon, where she's now enrolled as a sophomore. That makes her a Duck, not one of your more impressive mascots. We're hoping that someday she'll actually pick a major and learn something that will help her earn a living. In the meantime, she's getting B's while juggling a part-time job at the college bookstore and enjoying a fairly active social life. She met her current boyfriend, Jonathan, by accident. Literally. She backed her new Jetta into his Ford Explorer in a student parking lot. Fortunately, nobody was hurt, and they've been an item ever since. He's a senior, majoring in architecture, and we hate him less than the other boyfriends she's had.

Eugene is an eclectic user-friendly town. I like the fact that most things are within walking distance. We live in a white two-story house just outside the city limits, on a heavily wooded acre a stone's throw from Fern Ridge Lake. As soon as I saw the big wrap-around porch, I knew this was where I wanted to spend the rest of my life. Maybe I'll get tired of all the greenery in thirty or forty years, but I doubt it.

Jason was wrong. I don't miss the ad game and I don't miss Las Vegas. To paraphrase Paul Simon, "Vegas seems like a dream to me now." It's hard to believe that place is there all the time. Sometimes I think that as soon as we left, the man behind the curtain pushed a button and the town receded into the desert like the waters after a flash flood. I mean, there's really no reason for Vegas to exist, other than the gambling. If it weren't for the slots, black-jack, and craps, Las Vegas would consist of two gas stations, a bar, and a greasy spoon.

Pam likes Eugene, too. She's given up on the bed-and-breakfast idea for now. She's having too much fun running our own little charitable foundation, the Nichols Fund. It sounds more impressive than it is. Still, we're doing what we can, without going broke in the process. Once every couple of weeks, we sit around the kitchen table and sift through the endless stream of requests for money. Cards, letters, manila envelopes, stacked halfway to the ceiling like miniature paper skyscrapers. Most are from sponges, leeches, get-rich-quick schemers, and other assorted misfits. The wacky inventors are the best. One guy claims to have designed an engine that runs on hu-man gaseous emissions. (Farts, to you and me.) These, as you can imagine, hit the trashcan faster than an Angela Jackson in-your-face three-pointer.

But some of the appeals are deserving and a few are downright heart-breaking. We've already parceled out a college scholarship, covered some medical bills, and sent a kid to camp. Don't nominate us for sainthood just yet. I'd settle for *Time's* "Man of the Year."

When I'm not arguing with the family about who gets what, I teach an extension class at Lane Community Col-lege. It's for small business owners who need to get maxi-mum impact for their advertising dollar. Real hands-on stuff that works, not a bunch of theories and other crap from a textbook. I like teaching. It keeps me out of trouble and the students have to laugh at my jokes.

Jason and I talk every few weeks. He's living in a small apartment in Hermosa Beach, California, walking distance to the ocean. He claims he loves the hot-dog business, but I'm starting to not believe him. His buddies tell me he spends more time surfing and partying than chopping onions and squeezing mustard. What the hell, he can afford it.

And then there's Angela. She moved to Phoenix and traded in her nurse's uniform for a playbook and clipboard, taking a position as assistant basketball coach at a local high school. For the boy's team, no less. I'm sure they don't give her any shit. She and Clyde are going strong. I suppose they're "hitting it," or whatever they call it these days. The last time I spoke with her, she hinted there might be wedding bells in their future.

"You've been able to get past that name."

"That's not the half of it. He wants three kids. Clyde, Jr., Clydetta, and Clydene."

Pam came into the room right after I hung up.

"Who's that?"

"Angela."

"I'm sorry I missed her. What's new with her?"

"Well," I said, "she and Clyde are still an item, he hasn't popped the question yet but he's sort of hinted around, and she knows he wants three kids."

Pam's mouth fell open and she pretended to stagger toward the chair. "I can't believe you know all this stuff. There's hope for you yet."

"How about that," I said. "I think I'll make myself a snack. As a reward."

"You do that."

"So," I said, "where do you keep the cookies around here?"

ABOUT THE AUTHOR

Brian Rouff has lived in Las Vegas since 1981, which makes him a long-timer by local standards. He is married with two grown daughters, and a three-year-old grandson. This is his second novel.

The author can be contacted at the following e-mail address: brouff55@aol.com